T0311342

Sustainable Residential Investing

For investors from across the world, UK residential property is seen as one of the best investments available. This is for good reason. It has a track record of delivering strong, stable returns in a way that is relatively easy to understand and implement. The trouble is, the market has changed. The investors of the future value sustainability more than ever before. There is unprecedented and growing demand for Environmental Social and Governance (ESG) investing, now worth $30 trillion in Assets Under Management each year, around a quarter of all professionally managed assets.

The traditional goal of profit maximisation is being replaced. Investments must increasingly be profitable as well as sustainable: economically resilient with positive ESG metrics. Yet the UK residential property market – worth over £7.5 trillion – is lagging behind. There is very little clear, easily usable guidance for those responsible for a huge proportion of the market: private investors. The positive impacts of sustainable property investing – for profit-motivated investors, people and the planet – could be huge. The financial, environmental and social costs of getting it wrong could be catastrophic.

To get this right and to avoid the risks of getting it wrong, it is vital to understand:

- What sustainable residential property investing is
- What needs to change and
- How, on a practical level, you can invest in a way that is both profitable and sustainable.

This book draws on expertise from within and beyond real estate, provides a simple framework for updating your approach. It highlights common mistakes and shares advice so that you can avoid them. Ultimately, it's about answering the question of the decade: 'How can I invest profitably with positive impacts?'

Anna Clare Harper is a property investor, strategist, podcast host and author of Amazon best sellers *Strategic Property Investing* and *Building a Legacy*. She is a Director at IMMO, Europe's leading technology-led real estate platform, creating quality single family rental portfolios at speed and scale. Anna was named in *Management Today's* '35 Women Under 35' and *Bisnow's* 'Women Leading Real Estate'. She previously developed the strategy and built the seed portfolio for an HNWI-backed fund targeting a £100 million+ housing portfolio, worked on £2 billion+ transactions as a strategist at Deloitte and studied real estate at Cambridge. Anna is a TEDx speaker, hosts a leading property podcast and is regularly featured in leading publications, including the *Financial Times*, BBC and *Forbes*.

'As the UK emerges post-Brexit and post-pandemic there are some clear markets where investors are clearly now looking at the investment potential, residential is definitely one, but what is exciting is that this is now also looking at the potential for sustainable investment in the asset class that brings together the potential of People, Place and Profit. No longer are these mutually exclusive but can combine to deliver ethical investment based on robust business analysis. This book takes the investor on the journey of the potential of how Sustainable Property Investing in the UK residential property market can build a better life and legacy. The timing is now to change our mindset and this book sets out how we can make this a reality.'

– Amanda Clack, CBRE, UK

Sustainable Residential Investing

How to Make Profits with Positive Impacts from UK Property

Anna Clare Harper

Routledge
Taylor & Francis Group

LONDON AND NEW YORK

Cover image: © AerialPerspective Images/Getty Images

First published 2022
by Routledge
4 Park Square, Milton Park, Abingdon, Oxon OX14 4RN

and by Routledge
605 Third Avenue, New York, NY 10158

Routledge is an imprint of the Taylor & Francis Group, an informa business

© 2022 Anna Clare Harper

The right of Anna Clare Harper to be identified as author of this work has been asserted in accordance with sections 77 and 78 of the Copyright, Designs and Patents Act 1988.

British Library Cataloguing-in-Publication Data
A catalogue record for this book is available from the British Library

Library of Congress Cataloging-in-Publication Data
A catalog record for this book has been requested

ISBN: 978-1-032-05312-7 (hbk)
ISBN: 978-1-032-05309-7 (pbk)
ISBN: 978-1-003-19698-3 (ebk)

DOI: 10.1201/9781003196983

Typeset in Bembo
by Apex CoVantage, LLC

Contents

10 Summary/conclusion

60 Second Summary

For investors from across the world, UK residential property is seen as one of the best investments available.

This is for good reason. It has a track record of delivering strong, stable returns in a way that is relatively easy to understand and implement.

The trouble is, the market has changed. The investors of the future value sustainability more than ever before. There is unprecedented and growing demand for Environmental Social and Governance (ESG) investing, now worth $30 trillion in Assets Under Management each year, around a quarter of all professionally managed assets.[1]

The traditional goal of profit maximisation is being replaced. Investments must increasingly be profitable as well as sustainable: economically resilient with positive ESG metrics.

Yet the UK residential property market – worth over £7.5 trillion[2] – is lagging behind. There is very little clear, easily usable guidance for those responsible for a huge proportion of the market: private investors.

The positive impacts of sustainable property investing – for profit-motivated investors, people and the planet – could be huge. The financial, environmental and social costs of getting it wrong could be catastrophic.

To get this right and to avoid the risks of getting it wrong, it is vital to understand:

*   What sustainable residential property investing is,
*   What needs to change and

- How, on a practical level, you can invest in a way that is both profitable and sustainable.

This book draws on expertise from within and, beyond real estate, provides a simple framework for updating your approach. It highlights common mistakes and shares advice so that you can avoid them. Ultimately, it's about answering the question of the decade: 'How can I invest profitably with positive impacts?'

Notes

1 Gina Martin Adams (February 2021) ESG assets may hit $53 trillion by 2025, a third of global AUM www.bloomberg.com/professional/blog/esg-assets-may-hit-53-trillion-by-2025-a-third-of-global-aum/ [November 2021]
2 Lawrence Bowles (March 2021) UK housing value hits record £7.56 trillion high www.savills.co.uk/insight-and-opinion/savills-news/311889-0/uk-housing-value-hits-record-%C2%A37.56-trillion-high [November 2021]

Acknowledgements

I would like to thank the amazing people who have supported me with this book, without which it would still be an idea. In particular:

- Damien, Ruth and Ana, for their practical ideas and encouragement
- Charlotte and Rebekah for their fantastic contributions and critique – the best ideas in this book are thanks to you!
- John and Victoria for their unwavering support and enthusiasm
- Sylvia and Helen for keeping me going and keeping me (mostly) sane
- Ed and Andrew for helping transform an ambitious book idea into reality

Introduction

What you will learn

This introduction will explain:

- *Why you should read this book*
- *Why sustainable residential investing is more important now than ever*
- *Who this book is for*
- *About the author*
- *What this book is and what it isn't*
- *How it works*

Why read this book?

For many years, UK residential property has been seen as one of the most attractive investments available. It has offered investors attractive yields, growth and stability in a way that seems relatively easy to understand and implement. As a result, it continues to attract capital from all over the world.

The trouble is, the market has changed. Not only are profit margins being squeezed due to more regulations and more competition from investors and homeowners, but the investors of the future value sustainability more than ever before.

There is unprecedented and growing demand for Environmental Social and Governance (ESG) investing. This sector is now worth $30 trillion in Assets Under Management each year, around a quarter of global professionally managed assets.[1] The traditional goal of

DOI: 10.1201/9781003196983-1

profit maximisation is being replaced. Investments must increasingly be profitable as well as sustainable: economically resilient with positive ESG metrics.

The UK residential property market – worth over £7.5 trillion[2] – is lagging behind. Yet it is of crucial importance to us all and to achieving global and national environmental sustainability targets. Of all UK emissions, 40% come from households,[3] and 76% of our housing was built before building regulations required insulation.[4]

The positive impacts of sustainable property investing could be huge for profit-motivated investors, people and the planet. The financial, environmental and social risks and costs of getting it wrong could be catastrophic.

Real estate funds and REITs, like their counterparts across professional investment sectors, have been paying attention to sustainability for some years now. However, these institutions are only responsible for a fraction of the housing market. UK residential property is dominated by individual investors or small private companies: 94% of property investors were individuals in 2018,[5] and in 2016, 93% of residential property investors owned four or fewer properties.[6]

The trouble is, there is very little clear, easily usable guidance for those responsible for a huge proportion of the UK housing market: private investors like you. The business case for change, for you, is clear. Firstly, it's about improving your long-term returns and the resilience of those returns. Secondly, it's about reducing your risk. Shifting to a more environmentally and socially sustainable model of investment can help you to avoid the financial as well as environmental and social costs and risks of being too late or being behind the curve.

Many residential property investors are unaware of how significant the growing importance of sustainability will be for the values, performance and risk of their investments through the 2020s as well as for the planet, and they are unclear on how to deal with the issues at hand.

My mission with the book is to help change that and to empower residential investors like you to adjust your approach to align with the times we are in, so that ultimately you can create positive impacts whilst making attractive returns.

Why now?

The UK's legally binding commitment to achieve net zero by 2050 means that now, sustainability is no longer a 'nice to have'. 'Net zero' is a legally-binding national target that means that the UK's total greenhouse gas (GHG) emissions should be equal to or less than the emissions the UK removed from the environment. What it requires is to first improve energy efficiency (for example: reducing energy usage), then to increase renewable usage, then finally to offset any remaining carbon (for example: through planting trees to absorb carbon dioxide from the atmosphere).[7] This legal obligation is showing up in the form of new rules, regulations and best practices affecting all sectors that contribute to emissions.

The urgency to address the sustainability agenda has been highlighted by the 'high impact, low probability' shock of Covid-19, which has strengthened the case for prioritising people and the planet alongside profits and illustrated the power of collective action to tackle global problems.

Who is this book for?

This book is for the kind of investors I've worked with throughout my career: private real estate investors who have or would like to create a portfolio that delivers attractive long-term returns.

It is written for you if:

- You know you want to invest in UK residential property in the 2020s as a way to diversify, protect and grow wealth, or earn additional income.
- You know you want to minimise the risks you take and future-proof your portfolio.
- You care about creating a better financial future with positive social impacts and want your investments to align with the times we are living in.

If this sounds like you, read on.

About the author

Anna Clare Harper is a property investor and strategist, podcast host and author.

Previously, she developed the strategy and built the seed portfolio for a fund backed by a high-net worth individual targeting a £100 million+ housing portfolio, was involved with c. £2 billion+ transactions as a strategist at Deloitte and studied real estate at Cambridge.

She has published two Amazon best sellers: *Strategic Property Investing*, about how private investors can adapt their strategies and navigate the current complex market, and *Building a Legacy*, a practical guide to building a profitable, sustainable property legacy. She gave a TEDx talk on sustainable property investing. Researching and writing these books and this talk highlighted the untapped opportunity for more sustainable investment in the UK housing market, and she thought she should do something about it through her next book.

Anna hosts *The Return: Property & Investment Podcast* (bit.ly/returnpodcast), which has become a leading podcast in the property investment space. She has included insights from her guests – leaders in the sector – where relevant in this book.

She was recognised as one of *Management Today's* '35 Women Under 35' and *Bisnow's* 'Women Leading Real Estate'. Anna comments regularly in publications including the *Financial Times*, *Forbes* and BBC on property market trends and sustainable property investing.

Note from the author

Now that you know a bit about me, you may be wondering why I was mad enough to give up my weekends to write this book in the first place. I'll be honest: at times, I questioned it, too.

My work and research had highlighted a gap in the market for a clear, honest and reliable guide to how sustainable residential property investing might work for private investors and why. I decided to write this because, on a personal level, Covid-19 and repeated lockdowns made me reevaluate my priorities.

I realised that:

1 Life is short, and if you think you can make a difference, you should find a way to do it.
2 You don't actually need to have all the answers. With complex problems, often nobody has the answers (evidenced once or twice by governments globally since Covid-19 reared its ugly head).
3 There is more to life, success and business than money for all of us – businesses, investors and even politicians.

I believe that at the intersection of profits and positive impacts lie great rewards. The best forms of investing are those which generate a profit, keep risks to a minimum and have positive impacts on society. These investments are in line with the UN Sustainable Development Goals (UN SDGs), which range from 'Sustainable Cities and Communities' (UN SDG 11), which is about creating inclusive, safe and sustainable living and working environments, to 'Climate Action' (UN SDG 13), which is about adapting and investing to reduce emissions and their impact on the world around us.

What is this book, and what isn't it?

The work I do and the content of this book is about empowering investors like you to make the most of the opportunities in the current market. It's about investing in a way that is rewarding and profitable for you as well as having positive impacts.

The truth is, due to the fragmented, diverse nature of UK housing stock and ownership (which I'll discuss more in due course) and the borderless nature of the problems ESG investing seeks to solve, there is a limit on what each investor can do whilst remaining profitable.

The major changes will come from government action (for example: new regulations or grants, major collaborative public-private efforts, and innovations that fundamentally alter how we operate).

Most private investors will be responsive rather than leading proactive, independent efforts to tackle key ESG problems single-handedly. So this book focuses on the changes you can make to make a difference. These might range from proactively aligning with regulations to adopting new technologies. My goal is to empower you to make marginal improvements that improve outcomes for you, for other people and for the planet. If this book can facilitate a hundred, a thousand or even one hundred thousand × 1% improvements in performance in the UK housing market, then it will have a huge positive social and environmental impact (even net of the environmental costs of printing the book!).

To tap into the opportunities of sustainable investment and to avoid the pain of getting it wrong, it is vital to understand what sustainable residential property investing is and how you can shift to a more sustainable model of investing.

That's what this book is about.

It won't and cannot provide you with all of the answers, a simple answer or 'the right answer'. In this nascent field, there are no right answers. Only a sociopath would think they knew it all.

It won't cover what sustainable residential investing is in other countries. It focuses on the UK. Elsewhere, in particular in developing countries, the landscape is completely different.

This book is not a textbook nor a how-to guide for beginners or speculative short-term investors. Instead, it will focus on medium- to long-term residential real estate: buying, building and improving bricks and mortar assets for the purposes of renting them out and generating a secure and sustainable income stream. It won't cover commercial real estate; it will focus on the UK residential sector, which is unique in its make-up as well as its social and political importance.

It won't cover charity or the not-for-profit sector. Nor is it for investors who care only about making money, with no care for people or the planet. Investing is ultimately about making profits, and this book is about allocating funds profitably whilst delivering positive impacts or at least avoiding negative impacts. This book has commercial benefits for investors since it can offer a way to capture value and reduce risks. It also has benefits for local communities and the world around us, from improved affordability of housing to reduced emissions.

How it works

This book is designed to be a clear, reliable guide.

The first part addresses the context. It explains the basics of residential property investing and sustainable investing. It explains how the residential property market has changed. It explains what sustainable residential property investing is and why it is so important for investors and society in a way that is relatively easy to understand.

The second part covers what needs to change, including a simple framework for adjusting your approach, which you can use to guide your next investment decisions and how you optimise existing investments.

The framework includes strategic changes needed to your mission, how to revise your targets to align with the times we are in, and the trade-offs you need to know about and accept. This will enable you to identify the right kind of investments at the right prices. It will help you to understand what a good deal looks like, what to invest in and what to divest. It will also cover how your timeframes for investing and your payback period (the time taken to recover your initial investment) may change.

Then it covers operational aspects of investing, including putting yourself in the best position possible to align with current and anticipated policy changes. This part is about operating in a way that is professional and compliant, incorporating innovation and measuring your financial and ESG results.

At each stage, I've shared insights and expertise from within and beyond real estate, examples and common mistakes along with practical tips for how you can avoid them.

Each chapter includes a quick summary. There are takeaway tips throughout. If you don't have time to read the book from cover to cover, just focus on these.

Notes

1 Gina Martin Adams (February 2021) ESG assets may hit \$53 trillion by 2025, a third of global AUM www.bloomberg.com/professional/blog/esg-assets-may-hit-53-trillion-by-2025-a-third-of-global-aum/ [November 2021]

2 Lawrence Bowles (March 2021) UK housing value hits record £7.56 trillion high   www.savills.co.uk/insight-and-opinion/savills-news/311889-0/uk-housing-value-hits-record-%C2%A37.56-trillion-high [November 2021]

3 Committee on Climate Change (July 2016) The fifth carbon budget www.theccc.org.uk/wp-content/uploads/2016/07/5CB-Infographic-FINAL-.pdf [November 2021]

4 Institute of Historic Building Conservation (October 2020) English housing stock age www.designingbuildings.co.uk/wiki/English_housing_stock_age [November 2021]

5 Ministry of Housing, Communities & Local Government (January 2019) English private landlord survey 2018 www.gov.uk/government/publications/english-private-landlord-survey-2018-main-report [November 2021]

6 Ministry of Housing, Communities & Local Government (January 2019) English private landlord survey 2018 www.gov.uk/government/publications/english-private-landlord-survey-2018-main-report [November 2021]

7 UK Green Building Council (March 2021) Renewable energy procurement & carbon offsetting: Guidance for net zero carbon buildings www.ukgbc.org/wp-content/uploads/2021/03/Renewable-Energy-Procurement-Carbon-Offsetting-Guidance-for-Net-Zero-Carbon-Buildings.pdf [November 2021]

Part 1

Understanding sustainable residential property investing

In this section, I'll explain what residential property investing is and why it's so popular. I'll summarise key aspects of the current market context. Finally, I'll explain what sustainable residential property investing is.

DOI: 10.1201/9781003196983-2

1 What is residential property investing, and how does it solve investors' problems?

What you will learn

- *What residential property investing really is and what it is not*
- *Three common problems potential investors face in the current environment*
- *How property has, for many years, solved three major problems potential investors face*

What is residential property investment?

So that we are all on the same page, a definition of *investing* is provided as follows:

> putting (money) into financial schemes, shares, property, or a commercial venture with the expectation of achieving a profit.[1]

Residential property investing is simply putting money into real estate, with the goal of getting more money out in the future.

This can be through the direct purchase, ownership, management, rental and/or sale of land and buildings. It can also be indirect. For example, it might be via land banking schemes, property company shares, real estate investment trusts (REITs) or other investment trusts.[2]

DOI: 10.1201/9781003196983-3

What is residential property investing not?

Investing in property is not the same as home ownership

Many UK property investors have become 'accidental landlords': moving house and not selling the property they lived in or moving in with a partner and doing the same. Buying a property and living in it, like buying a car which you drive, is 'consumption' rather than 'investment'. Why? Unless you are renting it out profitably or can guarantee that the benefits of capital growth will outweigh the costs of ownership, it costs money to hold on to it. It is therefore a liability rather than being a profit-making asset that produces income or is certain to increase in value.[3]

Investing in property is not about speculating, making a quick trade or developing land to sell on

Some developers will hold on to assets for the long term. Some investors do seek to add value to their assets by building on their land or developing buildings. Generally, though, development projects and property 'flips' are seen as a trade rather than an investment. This is the case both in theory and in practice – for example, through accounting practices.

Property investments are not just a financial product

It can be difficult to trace the destination or impact of your investment when it comes to complex and impersonal financial derivatives, stock market investments or commodities. For this reason, some controversy surrounds many investments claiming ESG credentials. By contrast, property investors provide housing for real people, their tenants, who exchange rent for a home. Direct property investment and its impact are real.

In the current market, what problems do potential investors face?

Many potential investors worry about three common problems.

1 Losing money

If you've ever lost or come close to losing money, then you'll know you need a way to protect your hard-earned wealth. You don't want to have to worry about how you are going to maintain your lifestyle into old age or how you are going to provide for your children.

Losing money can be sudden. It can also creep up on you over time. For example, in the current low-interest-rate environment, by not investing, your money loses value to inflation.

It's a risk every investor faces that's worth trying to avoid. As Warren Buffet famously said,

> Rule number one: never lose money. Rule number two: never forget rule number one.

2 Feeling unrewarded

You probably hate the idea of standing still and not making progress. You probably hate knowing that you're making less than you think you should be making or less than you know friends or family members are making.

You want to grow your wealth, and you may also want to have a tangible impact on the world, something you can feel proud of. There's a psychological and a social element to feeling rewarded. It isn't just about money, and it isn't always easy to achieve.

3 Lack of confidence

There are two types of confidence that cause issues for investors. Firstly, if you haven't invested, then you have to rely on savings or earnings to cover your current and future costs. This makes it difficult to feel secure and confident in your financial future.

Secondly, if you have invested or are investing, you may not feel confident in the results. Even professionals who dedicate all of their time and energy to investing don't expect to make money all of the time. It's simply not that easy.

Many potential investors struggle to work out the right approach for them, to know what a good deal looks like, or to know how to manage their portfolio. They fear making mistakes that could lose them valuable time, money and sleep through investing at the wrong time, in the wrong locations, in the wrong assets, or in the wrong way.

The pain

All in all, many investors worry about missing out on returns they could, and feel they should, be making.

How does residential property solve investors' problems?

For investors from across the world, UK residential property is seen as one of the best investments available.

There is an emotional pull and cultural attraction towards bricks and mortar. It's easier for most people to understand because most people have some experience living in a home. It feels like a safe place to store wealth because it offers a unique combination of tangibility, trust and a track record of strong, stable returns.

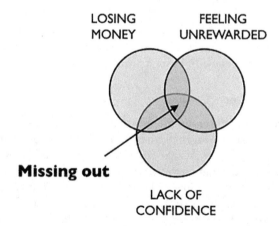

Figure 1.1 At the intersection of investors' three most common problems (losing money, feeling unrewarded and not being confident) lies the core issue: potential investors hate the idea of missing out.

In the UK, we are culturally obsessed with property ownership. This is reflected and exaggerated by the media, including popular television shows and regular articles in major news publications. As a result, individuals from all walks of life feel they can and should invest in property.

Owning property has come to be a signifier and determinant of success. For example, the *Sunday Times Rich List* is dominated by people who have made their money in their industry and choose to invest it in property. It is also the single largest asset class ultra-high net worths invest in, at 27%[4] of their holdings.

Owning and improving real assets and providing homes for people can be rewarding – a source of pride. It's a popular way to meet investors' goals of diversifying their investments, protecting wealth and earning extra profits. This helps to explain why, for so many years, it's been seen as a great way to solve the three major problems investors face.

Let's dig into each of these.

Protecting wealth

Residential property is seen as safe and secure: you can use it to protect your wealth. It feels, and historically has been shown to be, less volatile and risky. It's a time-tested way to protect wealth, meaning you may be less likely to lose money (although past performance is not a guide to future success).

It can balance the volatility of other investments. For example, many of the investors I've worked with also invest in the stock market. Since the turn of the century, the FTSE 100 has suffered seven times more crashes than the housing market. The largest peak to trough in house prices was around 22%, whereas the FTSE 100 has seen seven similar-sized sell-offs (2000, 2001, 2007, 2008, 2011, 2016, 2020). Volatility like this puts you in a precarious position if you need to sell at a bad time in the market and means your net worth can fluctuate dramatically over time.

By contrast, residential property tends to hold its value because of the fundamentals of demand and supply, which I'll talk about more in the next chapter.

Feeling rewarded – financially and socially

Property is also seen as a great way to grow your wealth. It delivers attractive financial returns in the form of cash flow and growth. It's also a source of pride: it feels great to have the kind of tangible and social impacts that come with providing and improving people's homes, whether you want to build a legacy for your children, impress friends or simply feel good about where you are putting your money.

So, it provides obvious financial and social benefits in a way that is tangible rather than leaving you feeling unrewarded.

Confidence

The strong track record of returns and the relative stability that residential property offers give investors confidence in their financial future.

As for feeling confident in your investments, unlike with, say, technology investments in the stock market, there's no pressure to predict the next hot trend. Everybody needs a place to live, and investors generally have some experience living in a property. For this reason, it's easy to feel confident in the investment case for residential property overall.

Areas can change over time, but demand doesn't tend to plummet overnight, ruining the value of your investment. So, provided you buy decent housing in locations people want to live, ongoing, strong demand for housing can help you to feel confident in your financial future and that you're not making a huge mistake.

It's worth mentioning lending at this point. There are very few assets that banks feel confident lending so readily on. Their willingness to lend, and to do so at a low cost to borrowers, illustrates how confident they are in the stability and returns that residential property offers. The added advantage of widely available and cheap finance for investors is that this makes it easier to grow a portfolio quickly for investors who have the right advice and access to deals.

The prize

Ultimately, investors want to protect their wealth, to feel rewarded and to invest in a way that they feel confident in, both in terms of understanding and implementation. They want to make the most of opportunities in the current market.

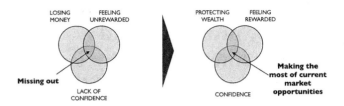

Figure 1.2 For many years, residential property investing has solved investors' three most common problems of losing money, feeling unrewarded and not feeling confident. It has done this by providing a way to protect wealth and feel rewarded that you can feel confident in.

So, property is partly an emotional choice. It's also a logical and time-tested one. It solves the three major problems potential investors face.

Summary

UK residential property continues to attract national and international attention. It is not the same as property ownership. It is unlike other forms of investing. It has an emotional and cultural attraction, and it's a logical solution for the common problems investors face. As a result, for many investors, property still feels like the best approach to achieving the outcomes they want. For many years, it has offered a solution if you want to protect and grow wealth and feel rewarded in a way that you can feel confident in and proud of.

Notes

1 Oxford Dictionaries – 'Invest' Definition www.lexico.com/definition/invest [November 2021]
2 Money Advice Service – Indirect property investments www.moneyadviceservice.org.uk [November 2021]
3 Robert Kiyosaki (December 2019) Rich Dad Scam #6: Your house is an asset www.richdad.com/is-house-an-asset [November 2021]
4 Sumit Mondal (May 2021) Where the world's ultra-rich lives and why most of them invest in real estate www.squareyards.com/blog/where-the-worlds-ultra-rich-lives-and-why-most-of-them-invest-in-real-estate [November 2021]

2 Why is the housing market stable, profitable and fragmented, and why is this a problem for sustainability?

What you will learn

- *What's driving strong past and future forecast performance of residential property: strong fundamentals of demand and supply*
- *How a uniquely attractive, simple and accessible investment has created a fragmented market*
- *Who is putting money into the UK housing market*
- *How diverse ownership and old housing creates a challenge for sustainability*

What drives property market performance?

At its simplest, fundamentals – strong and growing demand with limited supply – explain why residential property tends to perform so well.

Demand is essential

Ultimately, we all need to live somewhere. The essential nature of demand against restricted supply keeps prices stable. Stability is especially strong in the UK due to favourable, trusted legal frameworks, strong property rights and a deep cultural respect for our rights of ownership and control. Stability is also created by illiquidity. As frustrating as time delays can be when you're trying to buy or sell a property, this characteristic helps keep prices from fluctuating as wildly as they can in the more liquid stock market.

DOI: 10.1201/9781003196983-4

Demand is growing

Not only is demand for housing strong, but it is also growing due to:

- Rising living standards – more households can afford to make choices such as where they live, how they live and who they live with. It's no longer the norm to live with three other generations in a run-down house or apartment. Instead, households are choosing to live with smaller family units in higher-quality homes which they have selected from the many available or which they can improve for themselves.
- A relatively robust economy
- Demographic and social changes such as:
  - Long-term population growth
  - An aging population with people living alone for longer
  - Millennials and younger generations settling later or not at all

Supply is constrained

At the same time, supply of good-quality housing is constrained in the UK because we have a fixed amount of land to build on and tight planning restrictions, and building new homes is costly and takes a long time.

Research suggests we need 340,000 new homes built annually up to 2031.[1] We remain well below that level of new supply, with between 100,000–180,000 new homes completed each year from 2003 to 2021 and an average of 160,000 each year for the last two years.[2] This problem only got worse during the pandemic, and at the time of writing, the heady mix of Brexit and Covid-19 have created supply chain issues and labour shortages, slowing down new construction significantly. New regulations, tax frameworks affecting second-time buyers and tighter lending criteria introduced by banks are also restricting new supply from investors.

Past performance, forecast returns and stability

On the demand side, we have ongoing, growing demand for homes from investors, homeowners and tenants. This is set against constrained supply, limited by land availability, planning and con-struction timeframes and costs. The combination of growing demand against restricted supply has resulted in strong house price growth and attractive rental yields.

One often-used statistic is that since Nationwide began to track house price records in 1952, on average, UK house prices have doubled every 9–10 years. This growth trend is forecast to continue.

Rents also continue to grow due to ongoing, growing demand for housing and Generation Rent's affordability constraints and desire for flexibility.

'Generation Rent' is defined by the Oxford English Diction-ary as:

> the generation of young adults who, because of high house prices, live in rented accommodation and are regarded as hav-ing little chance of becoming homeowners.[3]

The struggle to buy a home has been exaggerated because easy access to finance has resulted in house rising faster than wages. As a result, although mortgages for homeowners are widely available, many people are 'priced out'. Many aspiring homeown-ers (especially younger people) cannot afford to buy their own home. Their effective demand is reduced, but they still need to live somewhere. This means demand for rental housing is higher. Outside of London, gross rental yields of 4%–8% are achievable and realistic. Rents tend to move in the same direction as wages, though there is regional and income level variation.[4]

So what does this mean? In many ways, there has never been a better time to invest in the UK residential market. Investor and homeowner appetite is growing thanks to long-term low interest rates and the absence of attractive, stable alternatives for invest-ment. Tenant demand is likely to continue to grow due to afford-ability constraints in a context of rising living standards, long-term population growth and shrinking household sizes.

These fundamental demand-and-supply dynamics are set to continue over the long term. As a result, yields are likely to remain strong, and growth is expected to continue too.

That said, property investing is cyclical, and values don't always go up. Cyclical factors include politics, the environment and finance, to name a few. The right time to buy is partly related to what you are buying. It is worth taking the time to determine the right strategy at the right time and using expert advice.

Diverse ownership because property is attractive and accessible

Strong historic and forecast performance, the cultural desire for property ownership and the fact that property solves our biggest problems (both for investors and homeowners, though we will continue to focus on investors) means property attracts interest from all over the world.

This attraction, combined with its accessibility, helps to explain why ownership is so diverse. Property is accessible because it's relatively easy to understand and because of the wide availability of finance.

Mortgages have become more widely available and cheaper since the 1980s. This has made it easier for investors from many walks of life to get their piece of the property market.

Who is putting money into residential property, and how is it changing?

At this point, it is worth addressing who is putting money into residential property in the UK now and how this is changing.

There are three broad categories of property owners:

Private investors

Individuals or small- and medium-sized enterprises – private investors – have come to dominate the private rental sector (hereon PRS – which covers any property rented by a landlord to a tenant). In 2018, 94% of property investors were individuals.[5] Most residential investors have four or fewer properties: 93% in 2016, though this percentage has fallen since.[6] The number of private owners makes sense because 90%+ of housing stock by volume is made of smaller opportunities worth <£5 million, which are suitable and affordable for smaller private investors. Larger funds struggle to scale down to this lower value efficiently.

Increasingly, private investors are either restructuring into a limited company and growing their portfolio as an investment business or rationalising and selling off housing. A new niche of 'corporate landlords' is emerging: investors with 5–500 properties who treat their portfolio as an investment business rather than a sideline hobby.

Since an important part of this book is about social impacts of investment, it's worth mentioning that there are social and generational divides between the 'haves' and 'have-nots' when it comes to private real estate investments. On average, landlords are older and less ethnically diverse than the general population. For example, in 2018, over half (59%) of landlords were aged 55 years or older, and the majority (89%) of landlords were white[7] and male.[8]

Institutional investors

Global pension funds through to REITs have a strong and growing appetite for UK residential property, in particular the PRS.

This has been catalysed by Covid-19, partly because the global pandemic highlighted the relative instability of commercial real estate. Unlike in commercial property, when it all goes wrong, we all still need to live somewhere, making residential property a resilient option. However, institutional investors have mainly focused on larger deals to date. Specifically, they have mostly focused on deals which they can control from end to end, such as 'build to rent' apartment schemes: blocks of at least 50 flats built for renting out under the same ownership and management.

This kind of housing has received much attention in the industry press in recent years. However, it still amounts to a relatively small proportion of housing stock. In fact, at the time of writing, all pipeline and complete build-to-rent housing amounts to less than 3% of the UK PRS by volume.[9]

Homebuyers

Individuals who own and live in their own property make up the bulk of the housing market.

The 'first-time buyer' (an individual or individuals who have never owned an interest in a residential property and who intend to occupy the property as their main residence[10]) agenda is a key part of many new government housing policies. However, affordability constraints affecting non-homeowners mean that existing homeowners dominate new acquisitions.

There is a generational divide affecting and affected by resource allocation. Younger generations are generally less able to afford to buy property. Older people are more likely to own their own home or to have property (and indeed non-property) investments. Once you have a property, it is easier to be able to afford your next property, which explains why so many people want to 'get on the housing ladder'.

The UK's diverse and aging housing stock is environmentally inefficient

According to the Department of Communities and Local Government,[11] in 2015, just 24% of the approximately 23.4 million homes in England had been built after 1980. The point here is that our housing is old.

UK housing is also inefficient from an environmental perspective. As Figure 2.1 illustrates, in 2014, 76% of our housing had been built before building regulations required insulation.[12]

Existing housing tends to be less energy efficient. On average, existing houses in England and in Wales that had an Energy Performance Certificate (EPC) undertaken in the financial year ending 2019 were rated within band D. This is lower than the current government target of having as many homes as possible in EPC band C by 2035.[13] To improve, we need much better insulation of old houses, including new doors, windows and lagging (pipework insulation[14]) across the vast majority of houses.

As Chris Goodall points out in *What We Need to Do Now*,[15] echoed by protest group Insulate Britain in 2021, UK housing

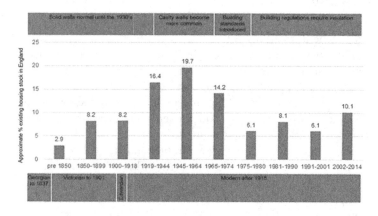

Figure 2.1 The age and environmental efficiency of English housing stock

has shameful insulation. The result is, if it's cold outside (let's say, 0 degrees) and you've heated your home to 20 degrees then turn off your heating, the indoor temperature cools far quicker than in average housing in, say, the Nordics or Germany. After five hours, your internal temperature would have fallen by 3 degrees in the UK, compared with less than 1 degree in the Nordics and Germany. This is a problem that will cost hundreds of billions of pounds to rectify. Fixing it could be a big potential source of employment once we have a suitably trained workforce.

Diverse ownership and old housing stock make it difficult to embrace sustainability

The fragmented nature of ownership, age, quality and variation of housing stock mean residential property in the UK is beginning to lag behind its potential in terms of sustainability. It is also lagging behind other sectors, both within and beyond real estate, in this regard. It is difficult for investors to deliver a consistent, quality product. It is also difficult for the sector to make meaningful progress towards a more sustainable model of property investment because the cost of retrofitting older less environmentally-friendly properties is so high.

In reality, the most effective way to solve the problems we have will be through further government action. More is required, and anticipated, from more stringent minimum standards to grants and subsidies.

Until then, investors must consider the environmental performance of potential acquisitions as part of their analysis. This is most widely measured by EPCs, which, although far from perfect, are a helpful indicator. Consider the building pathology and whether it will be possible to improve environmental performance. If improvements are possible, then you need to factor in the cost of transition to higher EPC rating bands (A–C) when deciding what price you are willing to pay. This may mean you need expert advice on how to improve the building's rating as part of your pre-purchase assessment.

Summary

UK residential property remains an attractive investment due to strong underlying fundamentals, performance and simplicity. Mortgage finance is also cheap and easy to obtain, making it accessible. The result is that property ownership and control is fragmented. Further, much of the UK's existing housing is diverse and aging.

The age and quality of housing stock and fragmented ownership make it very difficult to embrace sustainable investing. These factors therefore help to explain why the sector is beginning to lag behind in terms of sustainable investing.

Due to changes in who is investing and how it's done, now is a sensible time to reconsider how we approach property investment. There is an opportunity to consider what needs to change to make meaningful progress towards sustainable investing.

Notes

1 Heriot-Watt University on behalf of the National Housing Federation and Crisis (2018) 1 in 7 people in England directly hit by the housing crisis

www.housing.org.uk/news-and-blogs/news/1-in-7-people-in-england-directly-hit-by-the-housing-crisis/ [November 2021]

2 Ministry of Housing, Communities & Local Government (September 2020) Housing supply: Indicators of new supply, England January to June 2020 https://assets.publishing.service.gov.uk/government/uploads/system/uploads/attachment_data/file/922911/Housing_Supply_Indicators_Release_June_2020.pdf [November 2021]

3 Oxford English Dictionary – 'Generation Rent' definition www.oed.com/ [November 2021]

4 Office for National Statistics (July 2021) Index of private housing rental prices, UK: June 2021 www.ons.gov.uk/economy/inflationandpriceindices/bulletins/indexofprivatehousingrentalprices/june2021 [November 2021]

5 Ministry of Housing, Communities & Local Government (January 2019) English private landlord survey 2018: main report www.gov.uk/government/publications/english-private-landlord-survey-2018-main-report [November 2021]

6 Ministry of Housing, Communities & Local Government (January 2019) English private landlord survey 2018: Main report www.gov.uk/government/publications/english-private-landlord-survey-2018-main-report [November 2021]

7 Ministry of Housing, Communities & Local Government (January 2019) English private landlord survey 2018: Main report www.gov.uk/government/publications/english-private-landlord-survey-2018-main-report [November 2021]

8 Property Wire (April 2017) Some 40% of landlords in UK are women www.propertywire.com/news/uk/40-landlords-uk-women-new-research-found/ [November 2021]

9 Savills (October 2020) UK build to rent market update – Q3 2020 www.savills.mc/research_articles/254137/306754-0 [November 2021]

10 HM Revenue & Customs (November 2017) Stamp duty land tax: Relief for first time buyers www.gov.uk/government/publications/stamp-duty-land-tax-relief-for-first-time-buyers/stamp-duty-land-tax-relief-for-first-time-buyers [November 2021]

11 Ministry of Housing, Communities & Local Government (July 2016) National statistics overview: English housing survey 2014 to 2015: Housing stock report www.gov.uk/government/statistics/english-housing-survey-2014-to-2015-housing-stock-report [November 2021]

12 Ministry of Housing, Communities & Local Government (July 2016) National statistics overview: English housing survey 2014 to 2015: Housing stock report www.gov.uk/government/statistics/english-housing-survey-2014-to-2015-housing-stock-report [November 2021]

13 Office for National Statistics (September 2020) Energy efficiency of housing in England and Wales www.ons.gov.uk/peoplepopulationandcommunity/housing/articles/energyefficiencyofhousinginenglandandwales/2020-09-23 [November 2021]

14 The Greenage (September 2020) What is lagging and is it worth doing? www.thegreenage.co.uk/what-is-lagging-and-is-it-worth-doing/ [November 2021]
15 Goodall, C. (2020) *What We Need to Do Now: For a Zero Carbon Future.* 1st ed. London: Profile Books (www.profilebooks.com).

3 Why residential property remains attractive, but the old ways are broken

What you will learn

- *The key political, economic, social, technological, legal and regulatory and environmental changes affecting what works and what doesn't in residential property*
- *Why investors must change their approach to continue to make profits from UK property in a way that is commercially viable, economically resilient and sustainable*

Market changes

Residential property is still seen as a great asset, but the old ways are broken. The traditional model of individual investment in the housing market is ripe for change for more reasons than a desire for more sustainable investment. Margins are being squeezed as a result of new regulations and more competition, in particular from institutions. As a result, now is a sensible time for investors to reconsider and reshape their approach.

Investors must align with the key political, economic, social, technological, legal and regulatory and environmental (PESTLE) changes, from short-term tax changes to long-term demographic shifts, to grow and manage their portfolios in a way that is commercially viable, compliant and sustainable. Commercial viability and compliance are a necessary baseline for investments that are sustainable, so it's worth considering the key changes in turn.

DOI: 10.1201/9781003196983-5

Political uncertainties and a more consumer-focused agenda

Politically, and indeed socially, perhaps the biggest change in the housing market reflects a wider shift towards a more consumer-focused society. The needs of 'consumers', by which I mean homeowners, potential homeowners and tenants, have grown in their political importance. Results range from greater restrictions on when and how evictions can take place to billions of pounds of funding for first-time buyer schemes such as Help to Buy (a government scheme providing equity loans to aspiring homeowners so that they can buy a new build home with a lower deposit[1]).

In this digital age, the policy agenda is heavily influenced by media pressure. Politicians know that property ownership has come to be seen as a rite of passage. Policy-makers have never been so keenly aware of how their ideas will create headlines. The ability to 'get on the property ladder' specifically, and housing in general, are highly political issues.

Another important political influence through recent years has been uncertainty and change, both nationally and internationally. The truth is, uncertainty is the only certainty there is, so this is not exactly a new trend. What has changed is that our awareness of uncertainty has grown. News now travels across the world at the click of a button. Even after the impact of Covid-19, which is said to have encouraged nationalism globally, nations are undeniably interdependent thanks to globalisation and technology.

Major causes of uncertainty in the UK housing market have included Brexit and Covid-19. The Brexit vote, and subsequent years of uncertainty, caused many to hold off on investment decisions. Covid-19 initially had a similar impact until the temporary Stamp Duty Land Tax (SDLT) reduction. This was a policy measure designed to limit the impact of Covid-19 on the housing market and therefore confidence. It proved highly effective in reversing the slowdown of the housing market demand, although it did little to improve the reduced supply of new housing stock and lower valuations in some areas (e.g. city centres).

Political uncertainty causes some to delay their housing transactions. At the same time, it encourages the 'flight to safety' – a move towards investments that tend to hold their value, such as UK housing, which still looks like a relatively stable bet internationally. It has proved consistent and reliable relative to other international property markets such as Ireland, Spain, Portugal and the UAE in the face of comparable uncertainty and change. So, capital continues to enter the UK housing market from overseas.

Overall, the evidence suggests that uncertainty compounds existing property market issues rather than causing them.[2]

Economic realities – how long-term low interest rates and unemployment affect demand

The economy has a big impact on investment. Yet demand for housing has a relatively low correlation with economic demand, as we all need a roof over our heads. This is one of the most attractive things about investing in residential property.

I hope this doesn't last, but we can't ignore the potential impact of higher effective unemployment, in particular on younger people post-Covid-19. Many fear long-term economic, social and psychological consequences and rising inter-generational inequality. Higher unemployment creates further uncertainty and affordability constraints. In an environment of unemployment and uncertainty, all other things being equal, fewer people are willing and able to buy their own home. The result is higher demand for rental property. For investors, it is worth noting that providing locally affordable rental housing is a bit like providing a utility. It is countercyclical due to the essential nature of demand since demand is relatively consistent regardless of the jobs market.

Other important trends relating to our economy include long-term low interest rates, which continue to stimulate property demand. Capital is easily available, and investors have a strong demand for yields that exceed the base rate. This low-base-rate environment is likely to stay for much of the 2020s. Why?

• Economically, we measure success in terms of growth and use expansionary monetary policy to achieve that.

- In the aftermath of Covid-19, we now have so much national debt that we cannot afford to pay higher interest rates on it.
- Letting inflation increase helps the government to inflate some of that debt away.

Low interest rates not only make borrowing cheap, but they also make income-focused investments increasingly attractive. This is because the alternative, not investing, generates no returns at all and means your money loses value to inflation. This is the problem with cash ISAs, which allow you to save money without interest received being liable for tax. The low rates paid mean that regardless of the tax benefits, in recent years, you would have ended up losing value to inflation by allocating capital to a cash ISA.[3]

International uncertainties and relative interest rate changes are also a major driver of UK housing market trends. These affect international demand. They can change rapidly in response to confidence internationally and in the UK and relative inflation and interest rates. Since this is not an economics textbook, and any comment I make risks being out of date by the time this book is published, I'll leave commentary on the future of exchange rates and interest rates to others. The point is that international capital flows are changeable in response to economic performance elsewhere as well as in the UK. As a result, there are key drivers of the residential market in the UK that are totally unrelated to local demand. This is most obvious in urban markets such as London, Manchester and Liverpool, which have globally-renowned 'brands'.

Economic uncertainty, like political uncertainty, is both reflective of and driven by sentiment, specifically consumer and investor confidence. It has a knock-on effect on the housing market in the absence of policy intervention.

Social trends – the impacts of demographic changes and affordability constraints

It's difficult to neatly summarise the complex social trends and changes in a post-Covid-19 world. Long-term urbanisation was followed by an exodus from cities. Rising loneliness and health trends also play a part alongside longer-term, more evident population- and generation-wide shifts.

Two social trends in particular affect living decisions and therefore property investment strategies that work: long-term demographic changes and affordability constraints.

Firstly, population growth, demographic changes and preferences mean there are more smaller households and a higher demand for housing. The number of families in the UK increased by 7.4% in the ten years to 2020.[4] Household sizes are shrinking, compounded by a higher divorce rate and healthcare improvements that mean people are living longer.[5] The result is increased demand for housing. This has pushed prices and rents up since supply of housing is constrained.

Secondly, affordability is constraining homeownership and investment, particularly for younger generations. Average house prices have risen from being around five times higher than people's income in 2002 to almost eight times by 2018.[6] In 2018, the average single first-time buyer needed ten years to save a 15% deposit for a property (and significantly longer in London[7]). It's no surprise that in the twenty years to 2018, the proportion of younger people (25–34) owning their own home fell from 48% to 28%.[8]

More broadly, younger people are – due to choice or necessity – settling down later. They have come to value flexible access to premium features, such as a concierge or gym, over the less affordable and less flexible responsibility and burden of property ownership. The trend of access over ownership[9] encompasses transport (for example, using Uber rather than owning a car) through to housing. Younger people are less likely to buy as homeowners or investors and more likely to rent.

Demographic changes and the associated affordability constraints create continued and growing demand for rental housing. This improves the potential returns to well-located, well-priced long-term rental properties.

On the investment side, our ageing population also creates more competition for yield-focused investments. Pension funds are becoming the most powerful investors globally in absolute and relative terms and have a growing appetite for stable, income-producing assets. The requirement for yield from these powerful, sophisticated investors has been exaggerated thanks to compulsory pension contributions.[10] UK PRS housing is now one of the fastest-growing and most attractive investments for major global pension funds seeking yield and long-term stability. It has doubled in size to 20.3% households, now worth £1.5 trillion.[11] Historically, institutions have wanted the stability, yield and growth which residential property offers. However, they struggled to access it as they are unable to scale down to access the 90%+ of available stock that is worth <£5 million.

The general point is that with huge sums coming into the UK PRS, private investors face increasing competition – for assets and in terms of housing standards.

Covid-19 catalysed the shift of institutional investment in the PRS because it has performed so well, with an average of 97% rent collection versus below 50% in many parts of the commercial property market. This is expected to continue to grow in the 2020s, evidenced by how much capital is being raised for investments in the sector.[12]

To summarise, demographic changes, affordability constraints and rising living standards are increasing demand for affordable housing. People living longer increases demand for yield-focused investments.

Technological – advances improve the potential efficiency, accessibility and sustainability of investment

Technology is opening up access in the property market as well as increasing efficiency and quality for cost. Proptech and innovation have grown exponentially in their impact, often at little or no cost to the user. Online listing portals, such as Zoopla and Rightmove, have opened up access to opportunities and data. More digitised processes, such as customer relationship management software, are making management easier, cheaper and faster. Digital and online booking capabilities like Airbnb enable homeowners to flexibly rent out space and mean that people can move around more easily. The growing impact of online and hybrid estate agencies and lettings services, data platforms and the tokenisation of real estate through alternative finance are improving accessibility to specific opportunities and information.

Increasingly, data-driven decisions can be made with limited human interference. Investors can find, research and manage opportunities and implement decisions from anywhere in the world. Investing can be as easy as shopping on eBay, via crowdfunding, peer-to-peer loan platforms and REITs.

Crucially, we have greater capabilities than ever to identify and manage the right opportunities, and to do so in a way that incorporates what data we have on sustainability, from air quality to Building Information Modelling (BIM).

However, expertise is required to source the right deals and implement the right technology at each stage of the life cycle of the asset.

Legal and regulatory – a consumer-focused agenda shifting power from private investors

There is cross-party political will to solve the housing crisis and make the rental sector more professional. The increased cost and administrative burden of staying on top of more regulations discourage small investors with a few buy-to-lets. Armchair investment is becoming less profitable, more challenging and more time-consuming.

As a result, many savvy sideline investors facing shrinking profit margins are choosing to sell their now less profitable assets and get out of the market, or to scale up to a size where the higher costs of being professional and compliant pay off. The proportion of landlords with just one property has declined from 78% in 2010 to 45% in 2018. The proportion of landlords with five or more properties has increased from 5% to 17% and is still rising.[13]

One of the biggest issues standing in the way of more sustainable investment is that most residential investments are owned by smaller, private investors. With the growing regulatory burden to contend with, this kind of investor has ever less spare time or energy to consider the social impacts of their investments.

Specific policy and tax changes affecting investors include:

- Changes to mortgage interest relief via Section 24, which have increased the tax burden for individuals owning buy-to-let property. Holding a property with a mortgage for a taxpayer who has a higher or nearly higher rate has shifted from being a profitable sideline business to a loss-making one. If mortgage interest was 75%+ of rental income on a property before this change, the new regime means the investor owning this property in their personal name will now begin to make a loss.[14]

- The SDLT surcharge, an additional 3% on top of the existing transaction tax, makes buying more residential properties less attractive. After the temporary reduction in SDLT designed to limit the damage to the housing market caused by Covid-19, with the surcharge, SDLT would be £10,480 rather than £2,800 on a purchase price of £256,000 (about the average for UK properties at the time of writing, using data from March 2021[15]).

- More rigorous lending standards from the Prudential Regulation Authority, which have caused friction on the financing side. For landlords with four or more properties, in particular if held in a corporate vehicle, borrowing is now more complicated and often more costly.

- Additional licensing requirements mean that strong and specialist local and national market knowledge is required by investors. There are more and more stringent local and national regulations. These range from national House in Multiple Occupation (HMO) licensing to the selective licensing of private rental properties in specific geographies.

- The Tenant Fees Act 2019 has shifted costs from the tenant to investors, meaning that traditional buy-to-let investments have lower returns.

- Alongside greater regulation of the sector, the financial and social importance of tenant rights is growing. At the time of writing, there are 168 laws and regulations affecting residential property and its management. New Health and Safety regulations (for example, tighter fire regulations post-Grenfell) reflect this.

- The new minimum EPC requirement of Minimum Energy Efficiency Standards (MEES) means many landlords need to spend money improving their properties before they can legally rent them out.
- Tax changes (for example, around capital gains tax) broadly seeking to limit intergenerational inequalities

This regulatory burden reflects rising living standards, the desire for reduced inequalities, and increasingly, the desire to protect our environment and limit climate change.

Regulations, including those reflecting our new priorities in terms of sustainability, could outweigh the impacts of area growth trends on the value of individual properties in the future.

There is still substantial work to be done through regulations, policies and public financial support, such as grants to incentivise investors to improve and retrofit buildings. In short, a lot has changed, and regulations play a big role in what works and what doesn't. There is also more to come.

Environmental – growth in importance of and attention on protecting the planet

Nationally and internationally, in the public and private sectors, the sustainability agenda has become increasingly important.

I'll talk more about the private sector, with a focus on the investment world, in the next chapter. The headline trend is, attitudes amongst consumers and organisations alike are changing. There is a growing acceptance that money and things are not enough if key environmental (and indeed, social) aspects of life must be sacrificed in their honour. We can expect further advances in technology, finance and measurement to align with our collective attitude change and significant regulatory changes.

On the latter, government efforts across the world broadly align with the United Nations Environment Programme (UNEP) support. This is focused on 'mitigation' and 'adaptation and resilience'.

'Mitigation' is about making the transition to renewable energy sources, adopting energy-efficiency measures, reducing air pollution, and accessing clean-energy finance. In short, it's about reducing GHG emissions in order to reduce the rate of global warming.

'Adaptation and resilience' is about integrating climate change into national policies and development strategies and identifying new ways to adapt to climate change (for example, preparing assets for the increased risks of climate-related damage from rising temperatures and extreme weather).[16]

Measures centred on both of these are needed following the 2015 Paris Agreement. This is a legally binding international treaty signed by 196 countries to limit climate change and its impacts. The idea is to keep the global temperature rise this century below 2 degrees Celsius above pre-industrial levels and to strengthen the ability of countries to deal with the impacts of climate change (for example, through finance and technology).

Following the Paris Agreement, the UK became the first leading nation to set a legally binding target to cut its greenhouse gas emissions to net zero by 2050. Our net zero target affects all sectors. It's relevant for property investors because building and operating real estate has significant environmental and social impacts. These include about 40% of the UK's CO_2 emissions[17] as well as other environmental impacts from biodiversity loss (a decline in the variety of living things that inhabit the planet, which can affect people and the planet) to air pollution.

In the words of the Committee on Climate Change:

> UK homes are not fit for the future. Greenhouse gas emission reductions from UK housing have stalled, and efforts to adapt the housing stock for higher temperatures, flooding and water scarcity are falling far behind the increase in risk from the changing climate. The quality, design and use of homes across the UK must be improved now to address the challenges of climate change. Doing so will also improve health, wellbeing and comfort, including for vulnerable groups such as the elderly and those living with chronic illnesses.[18]

This book is not about new property developments. However, it's worth pointing out how policies affect development. The National Planning Policy Framework (NPPF) is underpinned by the principle of 'sustainable development'. Environmental Impact Assessments must be carried out for all new developments, in line with the Town and Country Planning (Environmental Impact Assessment) Regulations 2017.[19] The NPPF directly affects what can be built (for example, houses with parking or cycle storage) and how (for example, incorporating measures to minimise damage to local wildlife).

For existing residential properties, the options are more limited. For now, one of the main ways regulations are being used to limit environmental degradation is through MEES, which I mentioned earlier – targets measured by EPC ratings. Since 1 April 2018, it has been illegal to grant a new tenancy on properties with an EPC rating of below E. Since 1 April 2020, it has been illegal to continue letting such property unless exempted.[20] These minimum standards are expected to increase over the coming years as the UK government strives to meet its legally binding commitment to achieve net zero.

Overall, investors are encouraged through policy to focus on properties that are environmentally efficient or that are easy and cheap to upgrade, as well as to consider environmental efficiency in pre-planned maintenance schedules at the time of acquisition. This often requires specialist advice from experts.

What is the impact of 'now' for creating the right political, economic and social contexts in a post-pandemic, post-Brexit UK?

The current context has had a major impact on how important we feel sustainability is. In particular, the low-probability, high-impact risk event of Covid-19 has catapulted awareness and action globally to tackle high-impact risks such as those related to climate change and biodiversity loss.[21]

The pandemic has illustrated the strength of political power, where it is considered a necessity, to tackle major risks. It also illustrated the positive environmental impacts of slowing down economically and socially. What's more, technological progress has accelerated. This progress became a necessity, and as they say, necessity is the mother of invention. It incentivised innovation to improve efficiencies in many areas of life, including through the rise of working from home.

Social (in addition to environmental and governance) issues have grown in importance. In the Covid-19-led downturn, sustainable businesses and funds have begun to outperform their more traditional competitors. For example, Fidelity International, which looked at more than 2,600 companies covered by its equity analysts, found that during the first nine months of 2020, stocks with higher ESG ratings outperformed those with weaker ESG ratings.[22]

Investor, consumer and government appetite and support for a more sustainable model of investment is growing. This has been catalysed by current issues, including how the UK fairs in the aftermath of Brexit and Covid-19.

What key trends mean, and why investors must reassess their approach

Due to political, economic, social, technological, legal and regulatory and environmental trends, and the impact of 'now', investors need to re-evaluate their approach.

The old ways of investing in UK residential property, such as seeing buy-to-let investment in your personal name as a side-line hobby, are now more costly and complicated for the type of investor who has come to dominate the PRS.

As a result, now is a great time to reconsider and reshape all aspects of investing, from getting the right type of ownership structure set up to developing a strategy that incorporates sustainability.

Summary

Residential property in the UK has changed due to:

- Political shifts, including the uncertainty associated with Brexit and Covid-19, and a more consumer-focused political agenda
- Economic trends, including long-term low interest rates stimulating demand and unemployment limiting affordability for potential property buyers

- Social trends, including demographic changes, affordability constraints and rising living standards. These trends create growing demand for rental housing. People living alone for longer also increase demand for yield-focused investments from pension funds and individuals planning for retirement.
- Technological advances, innovation and data, which create the potential for investment to be more efficient, accessible and sustainable, making it easier to monitor and manage progress
- Legal and regulatory changes, including recent regulations, shift the balance of power from smaller investors and sideline landlords and broadly align with a more consumer-focused political agenda.
- Environmental awareness and the growing requirement to protect the planet, including through the UK's commitment to net zero

Due to recent market changes, whilst residential assets remain attractive, the old ways of investing are broken. As a result, now is a great time to reconsider and reshape all aspects of investing, from ownership structures to sustainability and impact.

Notes

1 Gov.UK – Affordable home ownership schemes www.gov.uk/affordable-home-ownership-schemes/help-to-buy-equity-loan [November 2021]
2 Hometrack (July 2018) UK cities house price index – June 2018 www.hometrack.com/uk/insight/uk-house-price-index/june-2018-cities-index/ [November 2021]
3 Rupert Hargreaves (September 2018) The motley fool: Why putting your money in a cash ISA will make you poorer www.fool.co.uk/investing/2018/09/16/why-putting-your-money-in-a-cash-isa-will-make-you-poorer/ [November 2021]
4 Amanda Sharfman and Pamela Cobb (March 2021) ONS: Families and households in the UK: 2020 www.ons.gov.uk/peoplepopulationandcommunity/birthsdeathsandmarriages/families/bulletins/familiesandhouseholds/2020
5 Trend Monitor (February 2020) The structure of families and households in the UK https://trend-monitor.co.uk/structure-families-households-uk/ [November 2021]
6 Nick Woodhill (March 2021) ONS: House price to residence-based earnings ratio www.ons.gov.uk/peoplepopulationandcommunity/housing/datasets/

ratioofhousepricetoresidencebasedearningslowerquartileandmedian [November 2021]

7 Alison Blease (June 2018) First-time buyers need 10 and a half years to save for a deposit www.hamptons.co.uk/research/pr/2018/Time-to-Save-Deposit-2018.pdf/ [November 2021]

8 Maja Gustafsson (June 2021) An analysis of younger adults living with their parents www.resolutionfoundation.org/app/uploads/2021/06/Boomerang-Time.pdf [November 2021]

9 Ádám Osztovits, Árpád Kőszegi, Bence Nagy and Bence Damjanovics (August 2014) Growth of the sharing economy www.pwc.com/hu/en/kiadvanyok/assets/pdf/sharing-economy-en.pdf [November 2021]

10 Pension Advisory Service – Automatic enrolment www.pensionsadvisoryservice.org.uk [November 2021]

11 Lucian Cook (2018) Investing in private rent https://pdf.euro.savills.co.uk/uk/residential–other/report–investing-in-private-rent.pdf [November 2021]

12 Ed Magnus (November 2020) Corporate landlords muscle into rental market www.thisismoney.co.uk/money/buytolet/article-8913985/Corporate-landlords-muscle-rental-market-mean-market-tenants.html [November 2021]

13 Ministry of Housing, Communities & Local Government (January 2019) English private landlord survey 2018. www.gov.uk/government/publications/english-private-landlord-survey-2018-main-report [November 2021]

14 Centre for Economics and Business Research for Shawbrook Bank (2018) www.shawbrook.co.uk [November 2021]

15 HM Land Registry (May 2021) UK house price index; March 2021 www.gov.uk/government/news/uk-house-price-index-for-march-2021 [November 2021]

16 UNEP – What we do www.unep.org/explore-topics/climate-action/what-we-do [November 2021]

17 UKGBC – Climate change www.ukgbc.org/climate-change/ [November 2021]

18 Gemma Holmes, Rachel Hay, Ellie Davies, Jenny Hill, Jo Barrett, David Style, Emma Vause, Kathryn Brown, Adrian Gault and Chris Stark (February 2019) UK housing: Fit for future? www.theccc.org.uk/wp-content/uploads/2019/02/UK-housing-Fit-for-the-future-CCC-2019.pdf [November 2021]

19 Department for Levelling Up, Housing and Communities and Ministry of Housing, Communities & Local Government (March 2014) Environmental impact assessment www.gov.uk/guidance/environmental-impact-assessment#legislation-covering-environmental-impact-assessment [November 2021]

20 RICS – Minimum Energy Efficiency Standard www.ricsfirms.com/glossary/minimum-energy-efficiency-standard/ [November 2021]

21 J.P. Morgan (July 2020) Why COVID-19 could prove to be a major turning point for ESG investing www.jpmorgan.com/insights/research/covid-19-esg-investing [November 2021]

22 David Ricketts (November 2020) Here's how Covid-19 is fuelling an 'unprecedented' explosion in ESG investing www.fnlondon.com/arti cles/how-the-pandemic-is-fuelling-an-unprecedented-explosion-in-esg-investing-20201112 [November 2021]

4 What is sustainable investing?

What you will learn

- *What sustainable investing is*
- *How to integrate sustainability into investing*

What is sustainable investing?

According to the Forum for Sustainable and Responsible investment, sustainable investing can be defined as:

> an investment discipline that considers environmental, social and corporate governance (ESG) criteria to generate long-term competitive financial returns and positive societal impact.[1]

In layman's terms, it's about making profits with positive impacts, or at least without having negative impacts.

Sustainability is no longer at the fringe of investor priorities. It has risen up rapidly in our global agenda since the Brundtland Commission's 1987 definition of sustainable development, which aims 'to meet the needs of the present without compromising the ability of future generations to meet their own needs'.

According to USSIF.org, impact investing grew by 274% between 2012 and 2018. In 2019, sustainable investing reached $30 trillion assets under management.[2] Assets with an ESG mandate are expected to reach $160 trillion by 2036.[3] At least 22% of the total UK asset management industry is now sustainably invested.[4]

DOI: 10.1201/9781003196983-6

The rise of sustainable investing reflects a growing global desire to ensure that we pass on a better future to our children. It also reflects a collective recognition that the environmental trends described in the previous chapter and social problems described later in this book need tackling.

There are two major problems with defining sustainable investment.

Firstly, the wide range of definitions, approaches, methodologies, frameworks, strategies and 'best practices' can be overwhelming. This can lead to confusion and inaction.

Secondly, it is difficult in any sector, not least real estate, to translate high-level theoretical ideals and UN SDGs into pragmatic actions with measurable outcomes.

The point of this book is to explain sustainable residential investing in a way that is relatively easy to understand. So I've deliberately simplified matters in this book. For example, I will treat the term 'sustainable investing' as encompassing all aspects of ESG

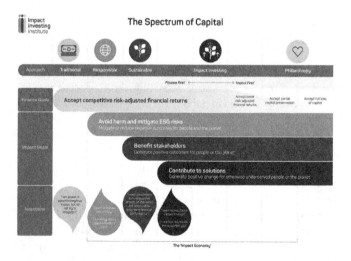

Figure 4.1 Choices and strategies in sustainable investment

Source: Impact Investing Institute – The spectrum of capital www.impactinvest.org.uk/wp-content/uploads/2020/11/Spectrum-of-capital-general-version.pdf [November 2021]

investment, covering issues from climate change through to diversity and inclusion. I'll include examples and illustrations to help you to move from a traditional 'profit only' model towards a more sustainable model of investing.

However, 'sustainability' is a broad and loaded term. For the sake of completeness, the literature does highlight differences in the different terminology and approaches. I've replicated one of the most helpful diagrams I've found to illustrate this (Figure 4.1):

How to integrate sustainability into investment

The big differences are around how you integrate sustainability, which have developed over time. The Investment Association outlines three key approaches[5]:

1 Negative/exclusionary screening or ethical investing

This is about excluding investments involving activities deemed unacceptable or controversial. For example, it would exclude investments based on gambling, tobacco, weapons or child labour.

This is a great place to start. However, one issue with this approach is that these investments generally create lower returns and higher risk compared to equivalent funds which have not been screened.

This approach makes sense because you are not selecting from a full set of investments; you can't optimise your risk/reward through full diversification.

2 Sustainability focus

The Investment Association explains that this integration approach involves investment in companies on the basis of their fulfilling certain sustainability criteria and/or delivering on specific sustainability outcomes.

For example, this might take the form of investments focused on achieving one or more of the UN SDGs, such as around climate change mitigation. It also includes 'positive screening'. This is where the investment manager looks for best investments based on

ESG ratings. This approach can open up opportunities for greater returns and reduced risk.

3 Impact investing

This is where investments are made with the intention of generating a positive and measurable social or environmental impact. For example, this might include a social bond fund that puts money into projects targeting positive and measurable social or environmental impacts. It might include private investments clearly investing towards a positive social or environmental impact, often in line with and measured against the UN SDGs.

The key here is being able to demonstrate that the impact is 'positive' and 'measurable'. For example, an oil company whose work improves our living standards and which invests in renewable energy may be investing in climate change mitigation technologies. However, the positive impact of its sustainable investment may not outweigh the negative environmental impacts elsewhere.

The good news for investors is that whilst ethical or negative exclusionary investing can limit returns and increase risk, the more proactive approaches of sustainability focus and impact investing appear to have positive impacts on performance or at least no performance penalty.[6]

What is sustainable investing not?

For many years, investors were purely profit motivated. Charities, not-for-profits and governments sought to solve social problems. Since the problems still exist, it seems it's time for the private sector to step in alongside socially driven organisations. It's time for individuals as well as institutions to step in and support existing efforts.

Unlike charity or not-for-profit, sustainable investing is about making a profit. Specifically, it's about creating competitive long-term financial returns. Unlike traditional investing, it's not about trying to make a quick buck with no care for others or the world we inhabit.

It is not about greenwashing. This happens when an organisation or individual makes people believe that more is being done to protect the environment than it really is[7] through unsubstantiated claims making their products sound environmentally safe or green.

Not only can this be misleading, but it has serious costs and risks for the environment. For example, a developer marketing themselves as 'green' because they have planted trees, when the positive impact of this far less than offsets emissions from construction.

There's a strong incentive to greenwash, because by being considered socially responsible, that opens up access to the aforementioned $30 trillion of potential ESG investment globally each year.

'Article 8' Disclosure Regulations will help to limit greenwashing for larger, listed investors, but greenwashing is still a major challenge.

In the words of Private Equity wire, 'Sustainable investing remains plagued by issues of governance and differing interpretations. Seeing past the soundbites and effectively judging assets against environmental criteria will be a defining challenge for investors – whether individual or institutional.'[89]

Summary

Sustainable investing has many definitions, frameworks and approaches that can quickly become overwhelming. It can involve investments focused on avoiding negative impacts, focusing broadly on ESG-related outcomes or on specific positive, measurable impacts. It is distinct from charity, 'profit only' investing and greenwashing.

Notes

1 US SIF – Sustainable Investing Basics www.ussif.org/sribasics [November 2021]
2 David Uzsoki (February 2020) Sustainable investing: Shaping the future of finance   www.iisd.org/system/files/publications/sustainable-investing.pdf [November 2021]
3 David Uzsoki (February 2020) Sustainable investing: Shaping the future of finance   www.iisd.org/system/files/publications/sustainable-investing.pdf [November 2021]
4 Susan Hickey and Phil Jenkins (November 2020) The Sustainability Reporting Standard For Social Housing https://esgsocialhousing.co.uk/wp-content/uploads/2020/11/SRS_final-report-2.pdf [November 2021]

5 The Investment Association (November 2019) IA responsible investment framework final report www.theia.org/sites/default/files/2019-11/20191118-iaresponsibleinvestmentframework.pdf [November 2021]
6 Patrick Norwood (July 2020) The main principles of ESG investing www.ftadviser.com/article/121232/print-view [November 2021]
7 Cambridge Dictionary – 'Greenwash' definition https://dictionary.cambridge.org/dictionary/english/greenwash [November 2021]
8 Kinson Lo (December 2020) How 2020 accelerates generational shift towards sustainable investing www.privateequitywire.co.uk/2020/12/08/293268/how-2020-accelerates-generational-shift-towards-sustainable-investing [November 2021]
9 Kinson Lo (December 2020) How 2020 accelerates generational shift towards sustainable investing www.privateequitywire.co.uk/2020/12/08/293268/how-2020-accelerates-generational-shift-towards-sustainable-investing [November 2021]

5 What is sustainable residential investing?

What you will learn

- *What sustainable residential investing is and what it isn't*
- *Why it is so important for society and for investors as a way to solve problems, improve outcomes and reduce risks*

What is sustainable residential property investing?

Sustainable property investing is, at its simplest, about making profits from property – buying, building and improving bricks and mortar assets – with positive ESG impacts, or at least with negative impacts minimised.

Prioritising impacts

'Minimising negative impacts' sounds a little loose. In fact, it is very difficult to completely avoid all negative ESG impacts. There is no perfect answer. For example, the supply chain of building materials required to solve the housing crisis undeniably impacts the environment and creates air pollution for people working in or living near production plants. It is necessary to prioritise some types of impact (for example, minimising carbon emissions) over others (for example, providing more affordable homes). Regardless of the trade-offs required – between financial and ESG impacts and indeed within ESG impacts – the idea is that sustainable investing can improve outcomes for all in the long term.

DOI: 10.1201/9781003196983-7

How sustainable residential investing can improve outcomes, reduce risks and solve problems for investors, people and the planet

The size and growth of sustainable investing makes sense generally and in relation to residential property because it can improve outcomes and reduce risks by:

1   Helping to improve outcomes, solve problems for people and the planet, and reduce the risk of social or environmental disaster, from climate change to widening social inequalities
2   Helping investors to solve their problems through achieving resilient long-term profits and reducing risk in their portfolios

Better social and environmental outcomes and reduced risk of disaster

Good sustainable property investment helps solve major socio-economic problems and reduces the cost of their impact, including:

*   **The housing crisis** – a shortage of quality, affordable homes affecting 8 million (nearly 1 in 7) people in the UK, as outlined in Figure 5.1.[1]
*   **Poverty** – when your resources are well below your minimum needs, facing insecurity, uncertainty, not being able to heat your home, pay your rent or buy the essentials for your children. Prior to Covid-19, this was said to affect 14 million people in the UK,[2] though unfortunately, this figure is thought to have risen to over 15 million people through the pandemic.[3]
*   **Climate change** – changes in the earth's climate, especially the gradual rise in temperature caused by high levels of carbon dioxide and other gases,[4] with negative impacts in the UK ranging from flooding to reduced agricultural production, heatwaves and forest fires and rising respiratory infections in children and older people[5] due to homes not being adapted suitably to new weather patterns.

The ESG Social Housing Working Group summarises how more sustainable investments can improve outcomes and reduce risks in ways that align with many of the UN SDGs, for example:

*People may experience more than one of these problems with their home, therefore the totals of each problem cannot be directly combined to create the overall total.

Figure 5.1 Breakdown of housing situation 2020

Source: National Housing Federation (NHF), https://housing.org.uk/resources/people-in-housing-need/, People in Housing Need, September 2020.

'Access to adequate, safe and affordable housing' is a core target for SDG 11 Sustainable Cities and Communities. But housing is not just about 'bricks and mortar'. Having a decent, affordable home is an important determinant of people's health and wellbeing (SDG 3), has a positive knock-on effect on children's education (SDG 4), can help people into decent work (SDG 8), can contribute to reducing inequalities (SDG 10) and can provide a route out of poverty (SDG 1). The social housing sector can also help reduce energy consumption and tackle climate change (SDG 7 and 13).[6]

Environmental impacts of carbon and the property life cycle

Since this is about buying, building and improving bricks and mortar, it's worth distinguishing between embodied carbon emissions, operational carbon emissions and end-of-life carbon emissions.

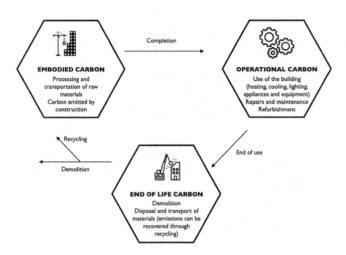

Figure 5.2 How carbon is emitted throughout the property life cycle

Source: Emily Williams (April 2021) The real estate life cycle and carbon www.savills.co.uk/research_articles/229130/313148-0 [November 2021]

Embodied carbon is the total greenhouse gas (GHG) emissions (often simplified to 'carbon') generated to produce a built asset. This includes emissions caused through the supply chain via extraction, manufacture/processing, transportation and assembly of every product and element in an asset.[7]

Operational carbon is what is emitted when the building is being used. It includes the use, management and maintenance (for example, the energy used to power a home).

End-of-life carbon is emitted when a building is demolished.

Embodied carbon accounts for an increasing share of the overall life cycle emission of an asset. It is expected to represent 74% of total emissions from new buildings between 2020 and 2030 and 49% of the total emissions between 2020 and 2050, according to a 2017 report by the United Nations Environment Programme Finance Initiative.[8]

These concepts are useful, but unless you are building from scratch or demolishing to rebuild, your main focus in terms of carbon emissions as a long-term investor will be on reducing oper-ational carbon and the negative environmental impacts associated.

Social impacts

Sustainable investment is not just about carbon emissions. The 'S' of ESG is also important. Real estate is responsible for meeting the basic needs outlined by Maslow in his renowned hierarchy. Real estate directly affects our ability to meet our physiological and safety needs.[9]

Some would argue that providing a roof over people's heads is a sufficient social contribution. My view is that the exchange of rent for a home is traditional investing, and it is not necessarily sustain-able just because it has some positive social consequences.

Instead, positive externalities can be measured by ESG criteria. These range from improving the affordability of quality housing for local key workers (public or private sector employees considered to provide an essential service, such as health and social care, trans-port, utilities and communication) to reduced emissions associated with heating homes.

How sustainable investing can solve investors' problems

The incentive for private individuals in residential property comes from how sustainable investing can help them improve commercial outcomes and reduce risks through facilitating:

- Improvements to cash flow and profitability
- Stable and growing values
- Lower investment risk
- Positive karma and marketing benefits

ESG and profitability

If you're used to investing in the traditional sense, you'll no doubt be thinking, 'That's all very well, but am I still going to make returns?'

The truth is, this is very much dependent on your portfolio and plans. Sometimes, for older housing with limited life left in it, it might make more sense to knock down the properties and start again. This has financial, environmental and social costs, which I'll go into more detail on later.

For now, the important thing to know is that yes, it is still possible to make attractive long-term returns through sustainable investing. Profitability and greater social and environmental consciousness are not mutually exclusive. You can generate profits and invest with a social conscience.

As mentioned, there is evidence suggesting the majority of ESG funds have outperformed their peers over the last 10 years.[10] However, since there is not enough data to draw clear conclusions on this yet in any investment sector, it's not a foregone conclusion. That's why it's vital to raise awareness, seek expert advice and understand the key concepts covered in this book.

For now, let's take a look at why and how ESG and profits could go hand in hand for residential property.

How more sustainable investments could improve your cash flow

Your cash flow as a property investor is rent less costs. These costs include the cost of finance, management and maintenance.

More sustainable investments may have better cash flows. This is because rents can be more consistent and maintenance costs can be lower.

For example, providing quality, affordable housing to the type of tenants who will benefit the most from this, such as young families or key workers, generally reduces void periods. Families typically stay longer. Key workers keep their jobs throughout market cycles. All types of tenants tend to stay longer when they know they are getting a good deal. These factors can minimise void periods. Families and key workers tend to take good care of their homes, which helps to minimise maintenance costs. As a result, both tenant types enable you to access long-term cash flows whilst supporting local communities and families.

Maintenance costs can be cheaper for more environmentally friendly properties – for example, through eliminating the cost of repairing, replacing and insuring gas boilers.

Provided that the reasoning is explained clearly to them, tenants may even be willing to pay higher rents for the benefit of lower heating bills that come with more environmentally friendly properties.

With the advent of new 'green mortgages', finance costs are becoming cheaper for investors in more sustainable properties.[11] Banks are more willing and able to lend on greener properties and to do so more cheaply, for two reasons. Firstly, they see greener properties as less risky commercially. Secondly, they are more able to lend on greener properties since government guidance encourages lending to greener properties.

How sustainable investments could make it easier to protect and grow wealth

A key goal amongst property investors of all scales is to protect and grow their wealth, often to pass on to future generations.

This requires a focus on assets that are resilient, which will hold their value for years to come, and assets that will be worth more in the future, which will grow in value over time. In residential property, consistent and growing values are attached to regulatorily-compliant properties that people want to live in, where they want and need to live, at a price they can afford. This kind of property is more sustainable both socially and commercially and can therefore be used to protect and grow your wealth more easily whilst delivering value to the customer (your tenant).

The commercial property sector is already showing clear signs of how the market prices sustainability into asset values through a 'green premium'. By this, I mean that tenants and potential buyers are willing to pay more for more environmentally efficient buildings. Higher sale or rental values are achievable, and the assets are worth more to the investor.

Conversely, a 'brown discount' happens when property pricing is cheaper where there is anticipated maintenance risk or obsolescence. The buyer factors in future capital outlays required and is willing to pay less for less efficient buildings. Put simply, there is a negative impact on value due to the property not being environmentally friendly.

In the residential sector, this green premium or brown discount is being catalysed by MEES, which I mentioned earlier.

Historically, capital growth has been driven by the shortage of housing supply and growing demand. It's easy to see how, via new regulations and laws, poor environmental performance of buildings could outweigh the impacts of this long-term trend. Less environmentally efficient properties are increasingly worth less whilst greener properties are worth more. This is a critical point affecting both values and risk.

How sustainable investments can be less risky

Residential property attracts investors because the amount of risk (or at least the amount of perceived risk) you have to take on for a given return is relatively small. The risk/reward ratio is low. This is helpful since ultimately, many investors want to build or protect a legacy to pass on wealth to future generations. Less risk makes this easier.

There are two major sources of investment risk and future cost that can be avoided by investing in a way that is more sustainable.

Firstly, there are the physical risks of climate change, such as flooding. For example, it may not be sustainable to build a property in an area at high risk of flooding or coastal erosion.[12]

Secondly, there are the transition risks largely associated with new regulations coming in with the goal of the UK achieving its net zero target. Since over 75% of UK housing stock was built before building regulations required insulation,[13] a significant proportion of our housing stock has high transition risk. Focusing on properties which do not have this risk makes a lot of sense since it is very difficult to quantify the cost of transition, but it will undoubtedly be expensive.

Regulatorily compliant, environmentally efficient properties that people want to live in, where they want and need to live, at a price they can afford will be more resilient through market cycles.

This enables you to deliver value to the customer (your tenant) with less risk.

How more sustainable investments create positive karma and marketing benefits and make you feel better

Politicians, consumers and investors alike want to ensure their children inherit a better future. This reflects the growing body of thought and activity seeking meaning and positive identity.

It's not just about feeling warm and fuzzy or being seen to be doing good, though it is hard to deny that there is an element of this in some camps.

Doing good, as fluffy as it might sound, creates good karma. Delivering a positive impact on people, places and the planet makes investors feel happier about their investments and enjoy investing more. It also encourages more people to want to work with you. Tenants want landlords, suppliers want clients and banks want borrowers who care. In short, there is good karma and practical marketing benefits. All other things being equal, this improves profitability for the risk and effort you take on.

Solving investors' problems

If the impacts on cash flow, ability to protect and grow wealth with less risk, and positive karma and marketing benefits play out, it's easy to see how a sustainable approach makes great financial sense. This is because this approach could enhance profitability and cash flows through lower operating expenses and voids, improve rental values and enable you to attract better tenants. It could boost values due to lower voids, higher liquidity (it's easier to sell a more sustainable asset), reduced finance costs and lower obsolescence. It could help you to feel and do good, be known for doing good or simply not be known for doing bad.

As a result, a sustainable approach doesn't just target societal problems such as the housing crisis, environmental degradation and inequalities. It also helps you to avoid losing money, getting it wrong for the market we are in and feeling unrewarded.

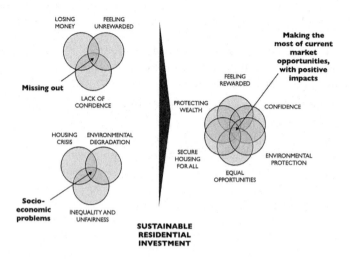

Figure 5.3 How more sustainable residential investing could solve social and environmental problems and improve results for investors if it's done right

Summary

Sustainable property investing is, at its simplest, about making profits from property – buying, building and improving bricks and mortar assets – with positive Environmental, Social and Governance (ESG) impacts (or at least with negative impacts minimised). It can help improve your profitability and cash flows and protect and grow wealth with less risk whilst you feel more positive about your investments. It can help solve problems socially, environmentally and indeed, commercially.

Notes

1 Susan Hickey and Phil Jenkins (November 2020) The sustainability reporting standard for social housing https://esgsocialhousing.co.uk/wp-content/uploads/2020/11/SRS_final-report-2.pdf [November 2021]
2 Chris Goulden (February 2020) UK poverty 2019/20 www.jrf.org.uk/report/uk-poverty-2019-20 [November 2021]

3 Hannah Westwater (September 2021) UK poverty: The facts, figures and effects www.bigissue.com/latest/uk-poverty-the-facts-figures-and-effects/ [November 2021]

4 COBUILD Advanced English Dictionary – 'Climate change' definition www.collinsdictionary.com/dictionary/english/climate-change [November 2021]

5 M. Mirsaeidi, H, Motahari, M. Taghizadeh Khamesi, A. Sharifi, M. Campos and D.E. Schraufnagel (August 2016) Climate change and respiratory infections https://pubmed.ncbi.nlm.nih.gov/27300144/ [November 2021]

6 Susan Hickey and Phil Jenkins (November 2020) The sustainability reporting standard for social housing https://esgsocialhousing.co.uk/wp-content/uploads/2020/11/SRS_final-report-2.pdf [November 2021]

7 Julie Hirigoyen (March 2017) Embodied carbon: Developing a client brief www.ukgbc.org/wp-content/uploads/2017/09/UK-GBC-EC-Developing-Client-Brief.pdf [November 2021]

8 Tom Walker (April 2021) Does an emissions scandal await the real estate sector? www.schroders.com/en/insights/economics/does-an-emissions-scandal-await-the-real-estate-sector/ [November 2021]

9 Dr. Saul McLeod (December 2020) Maslow's hierarchy of needs www.simplypsychology.org/maslow.html [November 2021]

10 Siobhan Riding (June 2020) Majority of ESG funds outperform wider market over 10 years www.ft.com/content/733ee6ff-446e-4f8b-86b2-19ef42da3824 [November 2021]

11 Mollie Millman (April 2021) What are green mortgages – and why are landlords interested? www.simplybusiness.co.uk/knowledge/articles/2021/04/what-are-green-mortgages/ [November 2021]

12 Bank of England (November 2017) Climate change: What are the risks to financial stability? www.bankofengland.co.uk/knowledgebank/climate-change-what-are-the-risks-to-financial-stability [November 2021]

13 Ministry of Housing, Communities & Local Government (July 2016) English housing survey 2014 to 2015: housing stock report www.gov.uk/government/statistics/english-housing-survey-2014-to-2015-housing-stock-report [November 2021]

Part 2

A simple framework for making sustainable profits from residential property investment

To invest in a way that is sustainable and profitable – taking into account economic resilience, environmental protection and social equity – requires three things:

1   A clear understanding of the market context and what sustainable investing in residential property is
2   The right strategies, targets and deals, which require an acceptance of trade-offs
3   A new approach to optimising, managing and measuring your investments, underscored by focused innovation

The first part of this book explained the market context and what sustainable residential property investing is. This part of the book shares a framework for sustainable investing.

*   First, it focuses on strategic changes: having a suitable mission, clear targets aligned with that mission and an understanding and acceptance of the trade-offs. This will enable you to identify the right kind of investments to make at the right prices and to know what a good deal looks like, what to invest in and what to divest of, as well as understanding the timeframes for investing and how your payback period may change.
*   Secondly, it focuses on optimising your operations: running your investments professionally and compliantly, incorporating innovations and measuring both numerical and ESG targets.

DOI: 10.1201/9781003196983-8

6 How to make the strategic shift from traditional to sustainable investing

What you will learn

* *The three things that you need to shift from traditional to sustainable investing*

    * A new mission and strategic plan
    * Clear targets aligned with your mission
    * An understanding and acceptance of the trade-offs

* *The key opportunities and threats affecting your strategy*

Rather than detailing residential investment strategies generally, which I covered in detail in my previous book, *Strategic Property Investing* (bit.ly/strategicpropertyinvesting), this chapter will highlight the most important strategic changes required for sustainable property investing:

* A new mission
* Clear targets that align with your mission so that you can invest (or add value or divest) at the right time and at the right prices
* An understanding and acceptance of required trade-offs (for example, elongating your payback period for the sake of a lower risk and more future-proofed asset)

Having these in place means you'll know what you're looking for and be able to identify what a good deal looks like, what to invest in and what, if anything, you need to divest. It's worth pointing

DOI: 10.1201/9781003196983-9

out that divesting doesn't get rid of the problem. However, it does get rid of your problem. If you sell to an investor with the capability to efficiently improve or knock down and rebuild a property, then divestment can help solve the problem rather than just your problem.

A suitable mission and goal

The best investments or businesses start with a compelling mission – a reason for investing – and a clear goal. Traditional investing might simply be about maximising income or making the most of the opportunities in the market from a short-term financial perspective: maximising your immediate, 12-month or 24-month returns.

In sustainable investing, the focus can still be on you as the main beneficiary of the investment. For example, you can give yourself financial independence through creating an income stream, which means you don't need to work, whilst feeling good about your investments. Alternatively, the focus might be on others. For example, creating a portfolio for your children or providing homes to vulnerable families in your local community as a way to generate profits.

This is the first thing that you need to address as an investor shifting from a traditional profit focus to sustainable investing.

Your mission will affect your targets and your strategy: what you buy, where and when you buy it and how you run your portfolio.

Adapting your strategy

Investors who see the greatest success over time start by having the right strategy. They don't jump in or make emotional decisions. They start with a clear end goal. They map out a logical, efficient path to it from where they are today, taking into account what's happening in the local and national market and how that affects value as well as personal circumstances. For example, are you aiming for net zero across your portfolio or to eradicate homelessness in your community alongside your profit motive? These two goals will result in very different approaches.

Your strategy for sustainable investment needn't be complicated. Typically, it will be long-term. It might involve:

- Buying and holding a portfolio for example buying ready-made buy to let
- Buying, improving and holding a portfolio of existing residential assets
- Building or converting and holding (for example, a commercial conversion or new build on neglected brownfield land, created for the purpose of renting it out)

Your basic strategy then simply needs to cover factors such as where you will buy, what kind of properties you will buy, who will be the customer (tenant), when you will buy, how on a practical level you intend to do this and how you will structure and finance the investments. These are defined by and will define your returns, how much effort you have to put in and the risk you take on.

Sustainable investments must be profitable and economically resilient. They will affect what geographies and assets you focus on. For example, if you want to provide key worker housing but don't have a way to do it in your local community, you may need to look further afield.

To be economically resilient, anticipated supply and demand must point in the right direction. For example, you would want to focus your investments in locations with good employment in growth sectors for economic resilience today. If you are buying a property that is currently in high demand but the source of that demand (for example, a local employer) has announced they will be leaving the area, then anticipated future supply may exceed demand.

Consider supply and demand and future supply and demand, including which sectors are growing and which are declining. In growing sectors, where do and where will people want and need to live? For example, do they want to live close to a hospital or 'outstanding' schools? What do and what will they want to live in (for example, two-bedroom flats or four-bedroom houses)? What is in high demand with limited supply?

You could focus on good-quality assets. For example, a minimum EPC rating of C will be higher quality than an EPC of E. Or, you could focus on assets which require improvement, and you can price that improvement in to define your offer price. By taking on higher risk to improve lower-quality assets, the expected return will, in theory, be higher to account for this risk.

Opportunities, threats and pricing

At this point, it's worth highlighting some of the opportunities and threats in sustainable residential investing. You can use these to guide your strategic decision-making.

Opportunities include:

- **Buying at a discount and improving building quality** – You can price in the cost of transition correctly and get the work done to improve buildings for less than the value of the discount. In the realm of building energy efficiency, there are opportunities for landlords to make relatively low-cost improvements (for example, setting boilers to the correct temperature, installing shading and increasing insulation). This is how, between 2008 and 2018, the proportion of dwellings in the lowest F or G bands fell from 14% to 4%.[1] There will be good deals with brown discounts to be had over the coming years to upgrade existing houses to A–C EPC bands. We've seen something similar in terms of how change is priced in in relation to fire safety. Many multi-apartment blocks were down valued significantly and rendered unmortgageable due to not complying with health and safety standards following the Grenfell tragedy. Savvy post-Grenfell investors have picked up properties on the cheap which require work to satisfy building safety standards and attain a satisfactory External Wall System (EWS1) certificate. This is an important form used by lenders to decide whether a multi-storey, multi-occupied building is safe to lend on.[2]
- **Marketing** – You can improve how you market the financial benefits of improvements you are making or have made to tenants to make the cost savings they will benefit from a

selling point of living in your property so that you actually get a return on your investment to upgrade a property.

- **Timing** – There is an opportunity right now to go beyond the minimum requirements set by the government. This makes sense if certain materials needed for improvements are likely to be in high demand later and could increase in price. The alternative is to be patient and wait for further regulations, grants and subsidies.
- **Energy** – Rising living standards are the reason behind generally growing emissions. These are overall a good thing. The damage is not because we are using more energy but because we use more dirty fossil fuel energy. The key in the wider market is getting clean energy to be cheaper than fossil fuels so that everybody has an incentive to use the former. The equivalent key in the property market will be getting cleaner, greener buildings to be more affordable than brown buildings and pricing brown assets right to incentivise improvements as a way of adding value. On the wider topic of energy, future policies could further impact values and create opportunities (as well as threats). For example, through the phasing out of natural gas and increased reliance on electricity to heat and cool homes. This is a key opportunity. You could make the shift to renewable energy – a relatively non-invasive and easy retrofit – sooner rather than later. For example, you could adopt micro-generators or ground source heat before the rush. Direct air capture and non-profit clean energy upgrades are also worth considering.
- **Incentivising tenants** – You can do what you want with the property, but ultimately, how your property is used and how good or bad this is for the environment also comes down to tenant behaviour. There are opportunities to incentivise good behaviour from tenants and opt for smart technology to limit negative impacts of less positive behaviour.
- **Non-invasive upgrades** – Technologies such as charging points for electric cars are getting cheaper, so you can consider opportunities like this which are less invasive within your property.
- **Divesting** – If you don't have the appetite for sustainable investment, then you can divest. Now is a great time for this

before the brown discount is fully priced into the market. As part of your divestment strategy, you could consider option agreements or 'rent to buy' for your tenants since the impact of costs required to improve a rental property can hit landlords harder than they hit homeowners.

- **Sustainable construction** – You could focus on building affordable rental properties using sustainable construction methods and materials.
- **Technology** – You could use new green technologies across your portfolio to improve how housing operates. These tend to get cheaper up to a certain point over time. For example, adding solar panels will be much cheaper now than in previous years and will pay off for years to come. However, this reduction in cost over time can be outweighed where demand for particular materials exceeds supply, so it can still make sense to take action sooner rather than later.

Threats include:

- **High cost to retrofit** – The cost of retrofitting generally outweighs the benefits at some point. I won't sugar the pill: retrofitting and improving old housing from an environmental perspective can be expensive financially, and it's got its own carbon footprint. Understanding when and whether this will apply to your portfolio can only be done when you have an accurate measurement of performance and the cost of improvements, as will be covered later in this book. At the moment, it's still cheaper to offset than to retrofit, and that is one of the biggest challenges. Effectively, environmental performance is an externality rather than being fully internalised into price.
- **Commercial implications of retrofitting** – There are practical issues around retrofitting. For example, if you need to do extensive work, not only is this expensive (I'm writing in the summer of 2021, at a time when construction inflation means pricing is 15% higher than this time last year), but it also means you'll suffer a void and perhaps need to arrange temporary accommodation for your tenant. This not only reduces your investment income but disrupts the lives of your tenants.

- **Limited capability and responsibility** – There's a limit on what smaller investors can do. Serious change needs to involve bigger developers and investors as well as government entities. This means more professional and better-resourced competition.

Overall, you need to do your best to ensure your investments are priced correctly, which may involve seeking expert advice. There are opportunities to improve and upgrade properties and align with regulatory requirements without damaging your profits, enabling you to make the most of the opportunities and avoid the potential threats. You may need to adjust your targets and timeframes, and you will certainly need to accept some trade-offs.

Updating your targets and accepting trade-offs

The reason it's so important to adjust your targets and understand your priorities is that there are many complexities underpinning residential property. The incentives of investors, operators, tenants and aspiring homeowners all differ, and these differ from what would be best for the planet. Further complexity is added by a growing regulatory burden and long-term growth in living standards and expectations.

For example, it is argued that the only way to solve the housing crisis is building more housing. This results in significant emissions and waste. Building projects, in particular those of a larger scale, need to be profitable. To be profitable, they need to be attractive to buyers with capital available. For larger developers, this often means building premium city-centre apartments that will quickly sell to overseas investors who have no intention of using them. So, even the most energy-efficient developments do not necessarily help to solve the problem of homelessness for aspiring homeowners or renters. Building new properties only helps alleviate the housing crisis if the end product is affordable and accessible. Even then, building energy-efficient homes, repurposing under-used commercial offices or retail or knocking down under-used commercial properties to rebuild still contributes to climate change due to the carbon costs of construction described earlier.

To navigate this, you will need clear priorities (and crucially, a clear priority since officially, 'priority' is a singular word), which you can only decide on when you understand the trade-offs involved for you and your ESG metrics.

As an example, a recent client I worked with – let's call him Robert – had £2.5 million to allocate to residential property. At first, his number one deal criteria was to maximise yield. This made sense since his mission was to replace the income that he had earned as a lawyer before retiring. However, when he learned about the growing trend of sustainability, he reconsidered his mission. He realised that he also wanted the portfolio to create a legacy that he and, in the future, his children would be proud of. This intergenerational legacy mission meant that he needed to future-proof his portfolio and consider its social and environmental impact up front.

The new mission affected his strategy. He had focused at first on high yielding ex-mining towns, which offered a double-digit yield today but had little growth prospects or economic resilience. He shifted his focus to higher-quality assets in growth areas rented to local families at affordable prices. His new mission also affected his set-up and structure. Rather than buying in his own name or in a limited company, he used a Family Investment Company (FIC) to achieve his mission of intergenerational wealth.

The targets he set changed from an 8%+ gross yield to a 4% gross yield.

'Gross yield' is the annual income on an investment prior to taxes and expenses, divided by the current price of the investment, expressed as a percentage.

Gross yield = annual rent/property value.[3]

It is useful for quickly comparing one asset with another. However, it doesn't take into account the fact that different investors and different assets will have different costs. One investor might have higher tax rates due to being tax resident abroad or lower maintenance costs due to industry connections or specific expertise. One property might be in mint condition with lower forecast maintenance costs.

'Net yield' is the income return on an investment after expenses have been deducted, including acquisition and transaction costs, management fees, repairs and maintenance costs, rates and insurance, as a percentage of the property value.[4]

Net yield = (annual rent − operational costs)/property value.

This is more relevant as a target, but it's harder to calculate. 'Return on investment' is the profit you make after costs expressed as a percentage of the equity you have invested. If you use bank finance and only have to put down a deposit of 30%, and if you include capital growth in your return calculations, then a net yield of 4% quickly expands to double digit returns. This figure is a useful guide for investment decisions. However, it can vary significantly with a small change in assumptions. As the old saying goes, 'garbage in, garbage out'.

Robert was happy to reduce his gross yield target because he saw that he could still make a net yield and return on investment he was happy with, with less risk and effort than he would have had with his original less sustainable strategy.

He understood and accepted the trade-off of gross income today and a relatively quick potential payback period in return for a more resilient, lower-risk, future-proofed income that aligned with his intergenerational wealth mission. His payback period increased. He accepted this as he was proud to provide affordable family housing with the environmental impact minimised.

The time horizon/payback period for sustainable investments is often longer, and the risks are often lower.

Sometimes, when you consider the trade-offs, there are hard choices to make. Are you happy to trade off shorter-term profitability for some aspect of ESG performance? For example, would you accept a reduction from a target of 5% net yield to a more realistic 3% net yield after all costs if you were confident that the investment would perform well over time and deliver positive social outcomes? Are you happy with trade-offs between different aspects of ESG? For example, will you prioritise improving quality of life for your future tenants or minimising the emissions associated with construction efforts in the first place? Do you care more about improving insulation by retrofitting an older property, or are you worried that this might create ventilation issues in the property for your tenants?

There are value judgements and commercial judgements to make. You need to go back to the priority you have decided will drive your mission then look at the facts of the case to make the decision. Unfortunately, there are always trade-offs.

Top tips

- Review what you really want, your mission, and make sure it aligns with the times we are in in terms of impacts for you as well as for people and the planet.
- If you find it overwhelming to work out what you really value and what mission you will prioritise, think about how you choose to spend your time and money, what things or people you surround yourself with, and what causes or projects inspire you – take a look at the UNSDG website for inspiration (https://sdgs.un.org/goals).
- Consider what you really want to achieve from your investments in 1, 3, 5 and 10 years' time. If, for you, it's all about maximising your profits over the next 12 months, with no care for others or for the world around you, then the rest of this book won't be much use to you.
- Adapt your strategy to ensure it will deliver positive ESG impacts. Get expert advice if you are not sure.
- Consider the opportunities and threats affecting your strategic decisions.
- Be clear and realistic on your targets. More sustainable investments often have a lower headline yield and longer forecast payback period as well as lower risk.
- Accept and understand the trade-offs between financial and ESG metrics and within ESG metrics.

Notes

1 Ana Slater and Jon Whiteley (July 2020) English housing survey: Energy efficiency, 2018–19 https://assets.publishing.service.gov.uk/government/uploads/system/uploads/attachment_data/file/898344/Energy_Report.pdf [November 2021]

2 RICS (March 2021) Cladding external wall system (EWS) FAQs www.rics.org/uk/news-insight/latest-news/fire-safety/cladding-qa/ [November 2021]

3 James Chen (October 2021) 'Gross yield' definition www.investopedia.com/terms/g/gross-yield.asp [November 2021]

4 Investment Property – Property Yield – Calculating property yields & return on investment (ROI) https://investmentproperty.co.uk/property-investment-resources/property-yield-calculating-property-yields-return-on-investment-roi/ [November 2021]

7 Three common strategic mistakes and how to overcome them

What you will learn

- *Common mistakes and how to avoid them, including:*
  - *Thinking ESG is a fad you don't need to worry about*
  - *Setting the wrong targets and timeframes or not pricing in what's next*
  - *Misunderstanding the trade-offs*

For you to avoid the costs and risks of getting it wrong, this chapter highlights common mistakes and provides tips for how you can avoid them.

Mistake #1: Thinking ESG is a fad you don't need to worry about

There are still plenty of people who think sustainability is a marketing fad that they don't need to worry about. It's true that there is a lot of marketing fluff around this topic, particularly in the corporate world. That doesn't make it less important.

The truth is, things are changing in terms of our understanding, culture, laws and regulations. ESG is not a fad that you can ignore.

Why it is a mistake

Sometimes it takes a shock to realise that something you thought was not important actually is.

Commercially, this might be about realising that the building you're about to buy or sell has been down valued due to its

DOI: 10.1201/9781003196983-10

environmental efficiency, that your portfolio is worth less than you thought for the same reason or that the cost of getting your properties into a rentable condition is twice what you anticipated because the windows are made of (metaphorical) cling film. All of these have happened to investors I've worked with.

On the social and environmental side, the shock might come when a person you care about finds themselves in situation where they can't afford to live near the hospital they work in. Someone you know may be forced into fuel poverty (being unable to afford to keep one's home adequately heated) just to pay rent in the city their children live in. Or you might stumble across a news article highlighting the true environmental cost of something as simple as building a house (for example, biodiversity loss and CO_2).

Our values, regulations and the market have changed.

On values, the tide is shifting. People of all ages are led by younger people who care more and are willing to put their money where their mouths are when it comes to sustainability.[1]

On regulations, ESG shows up in new regulations, policies and business practices. The result is a direct financial cost associated with getting it wrong. The UK government has set its stall out in pursuit of net zero by 2050 and a more consumer-focused, affordable and professional housing market.

Choosing to ignore this or is seeing sustainability as a trend that will blow over is short-sighted and unrealistic, both socially and commercially. The combination of a shift in values and new regulations mean the market has changed.

What happens as a result of the mistake?
What happens if you get it wrong?

Being a Luddite and resisting change rather than proactively incorporating innovation limits your ability to improve ESG impacts and make money in the long term. Commercially, there are three specific consequences to not taking this seriously.

Firstly, there is the impact on values and liquidity.

Secondly, there is an impact on your ability to finance the asset.

Thirdly, there is the cost of non-compliance or of getting your property to comply with regulations.

On values (how much you can sell for) and liquidity (how easy it is for you to sell), these are directly influenced by finance and the cost of compliance with regulations. I've mentioned the brown discount and green premium, and they bear repeating.

There are already 'widening rental growth differentials between more and less sustainable buildings'[2] in the commercial property world, which, as mentioned, leads the way in value trends as well as differences in ability to raise finance on an asset. Property buyers are more aware than ever of the environmental cost of their investments, making it harder to sell inefficient properties.

The impact of energy efficiency on values is partly because tenants, in particular in commercial properties, increasingly care about contribution to people and the planet and how that affects their brand. With increased competition for residential tenants from institutional investors (who don't just care about sustainability emotionally – they have a commercial imperative to illustrate their sustainability credentials), more regulations and bank guidelines favouring lending to greener properties, energy efficiency is likely to grow in importance over the coming years in both commercial and residential property.[3]

On lending, banks associate reduced risk with lending on a more environmentally friendly building.[4]

Conversely, bank lending is becoming harder and more expensive for less environmentally efficient properties. This exaggerates the impact mentioned on both values and liquidity. Guidelines for lenders reflect the need for more efficient buildings. In the future (although not at the time of writing), regulations are likely to be added.

On the cost of complying with regulations, you take on direct 'transition risk' by assuming ESG is a fad not worth worrying about. Transition risk is the (often unknown and potentially high) cost of complying with future regulations and the shift towards sustainability via regulations. For example, it might cost you thousands of pounds to add double glazed windows in your building. Risks for non-compliance with Minimum Efficient Energy Standards today include fines of £5,000 for breaches.

To get this right, you need to be clear about what you can control and what you might need to control. For example, let's say you buy a single flat in a Victorian mansion block. The good news is that such buildings are often built to stand the test of time structurally. The bad news is that your ability to improve the environmental efficiency of the asset will be restricted. For example, the freeholder may limit your ability to upgrade your windows or improve wall insulation. If you instead buy a freehold Victorian house, then although it will cost you to upgrade it environmentally, you will be in control of this.

To summarise, it is harder to sell, borrow against or rent out inefficient properties. As a result, the key point is that factors affecting living standards (such as size) and affecting environmental performance (such as EPC rating) can easily have a more significant impact on the value of your investment and ability to finance the investment than local market factors and valuation growth in the area.

Tenants don't want landlords, lenders don't want borrowers and suppliers don't want buyers who don't care about them or the world around them. If you're looking to grow a property legacy in a way that minimises hassle and risk, you therefore need to operate in a way that is sustainable and socially responsible rather than seeing ESG as a fad.

Top tips and how you can avoid this mistake

- Align with the specifics and the direction of policy. These favour improving environmental efficiency as well as providing safe, secure and compliant housing for people.

  - Look at EPCs when you buy.
  - Buy assets that will stand the test of time, or create a budget to improve them.
  - Consider environmental improvements as part of your pre-planned maintenance rather than letting this come as a shock.
  - Find out how you can improve properties you own.
  - Consider what this will cost, then budget for that, or divest inefficient assets and accept that the buyer may be doing the same.

- Manage risks.

  - Incorporate environmental risks that you're able to identify (for example, from EPC ratings) into your financial/investment calculations.
  - Seek quotes for specific areas of work highlighted in your EPC and building survey.
  - You can also work with an environmental consultant or specialist.
  - Cost these works up, and understand the payoff for improvements.

- Make sure your investments are priced correctly.

  - Refer to your EPC, suggested maintenance in your building survey and/or an environmental consultant to help you understand what you'll need to improve and how much it will cost. Factor that cost and any other transition risk into your investment calculations across your planned and existing portfolio.
  - This means you need to understand the cost of shifting to this new way of doing things.
  - If you're not sure, work with a specialist who does know how (feel free to contact my business – if we can't help you, we can introduce someone who can).

- Don't assume that just because something has worked before (for example, pokey flats in bad condition or relying on area-led capital growth), it will continue to work. Sustainability is likely to influence value, and you are taking on both transition risk and the risk of negative impact on values when it comes to selling.
- Be ready to accept a discount for environmentally inefficient properties you are selling.
- Accept that investing in a way that is sustainable takes work. If you just want a sideline hobby, it may be easier to invest indirectly via an REIT, a private equity or crowdfund platform which have the teams, technology and systems in place to take this on. There are advantages and disadvantages to each

of these options, and you need to do thorough due diligence before each investment decision.

- Manage your properties and tenants responsibly, or work with someone who will do this for you.
- Accept that you may not be able to simply rely on capital growth continuing in order to make your investments viable. You need to buy in areas that are resilient and manage them in a way that is compliant, professional and socially conscious. Not all property values grow when an area does if they are not aligned with the shift towards higher living standards and more sustainable living.

Mistake #2: Setting the wrong targets and timeframes or not pricing in what's next

Your sustainable investments will likely be longer-term, with a wider-minded vision than lining your own pocket. As a result, your targets and timeframes must change.

Longer-term funds and REITs tend to be realistic about the impact of investing more sustainably on their future income targets.

By contrast, in the private investors' world, there are still a lot of people selling hype and 'get rich quick' approaches or using marketing techniques such as 'guaranteed rents' and deals labelled 'below market value'. Add to this the strong yields and growth achieved historically, and it's easy to see why many investors approach property with unrealistic goals.

For example, it's absolutely possible to achieve a 10% yield each year if you're happy to take on risk or specialist, relatively high-effort investment strategies such as holiday lets that are, in effect, a business. But if you want to grow a low-risk, sustainable portfolio, it's likely that your headline yield target may need to be lower than this.

You may be disappointed in the 2020s and beyond if you are aiming to build a sustainable portfolio and instead:

- Focus on making a quick buck with no care for others or the world around us

- Assume you can rely on capital growth to do the work just because this has worked well in residential property historically
- Assume what has worked before will continue to work
- Fail to update your targets to suit a wider mission
- Fail to adjust your timeframes

Why is it a mistake?

It is a mistake to assume that what has worked before will continue (for example, relying on capital growth to do the work).

A more significant influence on value may be the new more consumer- and environment-focused political agenda. For example, I've mentioned that restricted lending is likely to exaggerate the brown discount for less energy-efficient residential properties. This same thing has happened in relation to another aspect of building quality, when lending was restricted for properties that failed to meet minimum residential property sizes. The result was that properties below minimum space standards became worth significantly less regardless of area-led capital growth.

Your time horizon and payback period for sustainable investments may be longer. For example, let's say you're buying a commercial building and plan to convert it to residential property. You could quickly and cheaply convert it into 12 micro flats (elsewhere described as 'rabbit hutches') with an EPC rating of D and a forecast annual 20% return on equity. Alternatively, you could spend a bit more on the property (for example, replacing the windows, improving the roof insulation and building to a higher specification, as well as doubling the size of the flats and adding electric car charging points in the carpark or solar panels on the roof), with an anticipated EPC rating of B. In this case, the ongoing return on your equity might be lower, say, 10% each year. Historically, developers have been known to cut corners (for example, spending money on interior design rather than genuine building quality, including environmental performance). This kind of approach will work less well for your long-term portfolio going forward.

Timeframes, targets, and transition risk are closely related. This is illustrated by the previous example.

The latter option means your payback period would double. You trade off a faster, higher return for longer-term returns that are more likely to stand the test of time. You have taken into account the need to create quality assets with better environmental performance.

The risk you take by choosing the first option is that you still have to spend to improve the properties later. It is much harder to do the work when you have tenants living in a property, so this could in fact prove to be more expensive than simply starting with the end in mind and pricing in what's next. The adjustment needed might be about spending more now and building with the future, and less risk, in mind.

The mistake you might have made, thinking in a shorter-term, more traditional way, is not pricing in the transition to a more sustainable model of investment that is being, and will continue to be, imposed via regulations. Compliance with anticipated regulatory changes is a helpful baseline for sustainable investment in the UK because the UK government is so proactive in its pursuit of sustainability.

How to avoid this mistake

To get this right, you need to adapt your targets and timeframes to fit with your mission, and you need to price in what's next in terms of regulations. This will help you to make easier investment decisions. For example, it would help you to choose between a recently developed, high-specification portfolio of family homes with a lower-yield and a high-yielding aging block of flats with low EPCs.

So, it helps guide you to the right deals.

It can also be helpful when you look at your existing portfolio and decide what to improve and what to divest. For your existing portfolio, if you haven't already started to consider how the shift to a more sustainable society could affect value, you need to start now. The direction of government regulations creates little doubt that environmental performance will impact your ability to sell or rent out properties.

What assets are you willing and able to spend money on to improve, and at what cost?

If you have the ability to control the asset, this will be easier, so if you have the ability to do so, freehold properties are preferable. If you don't want to do the work, perhaps you would be better off divesting before the brown discount is fully priced in across the market.

These decisions will be easier if you're able to make some calculation of the transition risk in your portfolio and potential acquisitions. This can be a complicated process, and it may require expert advice. The nub of it is that you need to consider the anticipated future costs of change and their likelihood rather than just considering your returns and what has worked before.

Top tips

- Assess your current portfolio and planned acquisitions with transition risk and the brown discount in mind.
- You need to focus on creating resilient assets for the long term.
- You can use regulations as a helpful baseline since the UK government is particularly proactive in its pursuit of sustainability.

Mistake #3: Misunderstanding the trade-offs

Back when profit was considered the only important motive for investors, decision-making was easy. Adam Smith's 'invisible hand'[5] (1776), at least in theory, guided resources to be allocated profitably and efficiently by and for self-interested parties. Everything else could be sacrificed in pursuit of profits. The world has moved on. Now, self-interested individuals and businesses have many more things to consider, including social value and environmental protection.

The trouble is, sustainable investment is hugely complex. It is a challenge to understand and accept the complex trade-offs involved. There are trade-offs between financial metrics and ESG metrics, and there are trade-offs between different ESG impacts, with unknowns at each stage of the way.

In an ideal world, sustainable investments would not require a sacrifice to profits. However, in reality there is often a cost associated, in particular in the short term. That might be due to the capital cost of building improvements, discounting rents to improve tenant affordability or spending more on management to improve resident and community satisfaction. Resiliency comes at a price. Sustainable investors would prioritise long-term, resilient returns over short-term profitability. However, there does come a point where the cost of an investment or improvement is no longer viable. This will relate to the target you have set. For one well-known housing fund I've worked with, for example, the minimum target yield is 3% each year. For other investors, it will be closer to 6%.

It's not just that you need to consider how profitability is affected by prioritising ESG impacts. Perhaps the best feature of sustainable investing is that it enables investors to focus on more than one benefit. This is also one of its biggest problems. In considering multiple areas of value (financial, social and environmental governance), investors necessarily have too many priorities. 'Priority' is a singular word. Juggling more than one can lead to overwhelm and inaction, and trade-offs are inevitable.

With all this to consider, it's perhaps unsurprising that many investors, from private individuals to professional fund managers, fall into the trap of not understanding and accepting the trade-offs.

Why is this a mistake?

Not understanding the trade-offs is a mistake as it can lead to unintended consequences, paralysis and inaction.

On unintended consequences, the trade-offs between minimising carbon emissions and reducing homelessness are a great example. Building new homes is a (rightly or wrongly) widely accepted solution to the housing crisis. At the same time, buildings and construction are some of the most damaging pursuits out there. Buildings are responsible for approximately 40% of the UK's CO_2 emissions.[6] Construction is responsible for 10% of UK carbon emissions and directly influences 47% of all national emissions.[7]

On paralysis and inaction, it is possible to go round in circles – paralysis by analysis – in relation to how impacts are prioritised and what trade-offs are made. That doesn't help anyone either since no decision is still a decision.

There is no right answer. Whilst this might seem a weak point to make, it is an important one. When there is no right answer, we tend to do the things that feel most comfortable, easiest or like the least bad options. As an individual, you need to decide what trade-offs you are willing to accept, and it would be a mistake not to consider this before you invest.

Getting this right is important since it impacts our shared future and legacy and your financial results.

How can we avoid this mistake?

There are two ways of minimising the negative impacts of inevitable trade-offs and maximising the ESG impacts of your investments.

Firstly, it is about understanding those trade-offs and making conscious, strategic decisions.

Secondly it is about the operational side of things, for example using technological advances to minimise the need for trade-offs.

Making conscious decisions about trade-offs

On the first – understanding and making conscious, strategic decisions – to some extent, trade-offs are inevitable in sustainable investing.

For example, should we prioritise minimising emissions or delivering more quality accommodation? Should we prioritise place-making or affordability? Should we prioritise worrying about overall economic and social confidence or reduced affordability of homes? This last trade-off is what helped policy-makers to choose a temporary reduction in SDLT, to stave off the worst of the impact of Covid-19 on the housing market and therefore confidence, despite knowing the strong possibility that it would increase house prices and therefore reduce affordability.

A utilitarian approach to ESG investing would advocate 'the greatest amount of good for the greatest number of people'. However, a philosophical approach doesn't really help individual investors take action.

The 'greater good' is most affected by minimising climate change in line with the UN SDG 13, 'Take urgent action to combat climate change and its impacts'. This is because climate change knows no borders. But it's complicated. None of us and all of us are responsible for and affected directly by marginal improvements to protect the environment. And, as we have seen on a global scale, some countries and organisations are more willing to make sacrifices to combat climate change – whether due to judgements around 'equity' in developing countries or due to protectionism, as we saw under Trump's reign in the USA. Not all nations are genuinely putting in the effort required to achieve net zero globally or to reduce climate change in line with the Paris Agreement.

Trade-offs are inherently political. What will win votes for politicians, earn favour and praise within an organisation or convince your children that you are doing 'the right thing'? This reputational aspect is important for business in a world where news spreads at the click of a button and we are all more socially aware. Would you rather be known for investing in the residential property equivalent of Shell, allegedly Britain's most hated company, or Apple, one of its best-loved brands?[8]

Politically as a country, we need to prioritise both quality, affordable housing supply (since safe, secure housing is a basic human right) and the environment. Some would argue it is easier to focus on political, nationally-focused problems and solutions such as building more houses as a means to improve affordability and ownership for first-time buyers, not least because housing is considered such a basic right. However, who is to say that this is the right approach?

The truth is, the reasons and rationale behind strategic decisions are inherently subjective. Decisions are necessarily made on the basis of value judgments about what is most important. There is no right answer. This is why there is no one 'correct' strategy for sustainable property investment. The mistake to avoid is making decisions without being aware of and accepting the trade-offs.

Ultimately, to avoid inaction, overwhelming yourself or endless philosophical discussions ahead of impactful actions, as an individual, you need to decide YOUR priority and what trade-offs you are willing to accept. It is not a perfect system, but since action is better than inaction, perhaps the best approach for individual investors is to consider:

1   Your values – what you actually care about
2   What you can deliver – your capabilities
3   What you can measure – since if you can't measure, you can't manage progress
4   What will make you feel good and what others around you will feel good about so that there is an incentive. Using ESG as a marketing tool might sound cynical, but realistically, without incentives, it simply won't work, and reputation is important – with suppliers, creditors, investors and tenants.

Improving operational costs to minimise the need for trade-offs

On the operational aspects of investing, there are two key areas which help:

1   Minimum standards based on regulatory requirements
2   Technology – which is a game changer for achieving more with less and minimising the impact of trade-offs

Regulatory standards as a baseline

In relation to policy, new regulations that impact investors in residential property may be costly for investors to comply with, but they also have major social and environmental benefits. I mentioned earlier that in the UK, although governments and policy specifics do change, the overall direction of policy is in pursuit of environmental sustainability. The attitude to regulating for sustainability is proactive, exemplified by our early commitment to net zero by 2050.

Therefore, regardless of the main social or environmental impact you want to have, regulatory compliance is a helpful minimum baseline which helps limit the inevitable trade-offs.

For example, new required minimum standards for EPCs mean that even if you have prioritised the affordability of the properties you own, there is a legal imperative to meet a minimum legal standard. Policies limiting eviction from landlords who have not responded to tenant maintenance requests are another example. Legal requirements are stringent. If all you do is meet them and treat your tenants how you would want your friends and family to be treated, with no further proactive effort, this is arguably still a huge step on the way to more sustainable investment.

Using technology to minimise the need for trade-offs

The need for trade-offs can be reduced as our capabilities improve, thanks to technology. For example, modular construction enables cheaper, faster and more environmentally efficient supply of new housing. The result is, in theory at least, we need not make the same trade-offs when using such techniques.

IoT platforms are another example designed to track and minimise the running costs of a building via lighting, heating and air conditioning monitoring and control. One problem with such new technologies is their obsolescence risk. This is the risk that a process, product or technology used or produced by a company will become obsolete and thus no longer competitive in the marketplace.[9] It's happening faster as technology evolves – the velocity of obsolescence is increasing.

That said, with new technology and innovation, we open up the possibility that we can improve on the age-old project management imperative of picking two from cheap, fast or good, illustrated in Figure 7.1.

We'll talk more about using technology to improve outcomes later. For now, the main point to note is that one way to minimise the need for trade-offs is to improve our capabilities. This requires innovation, and it requires uptake by investors.

Top tips

- Be clear about your priorities. For example, select just one priority on top of regulatory compliance to avoid overwhelming yourself and inaction.

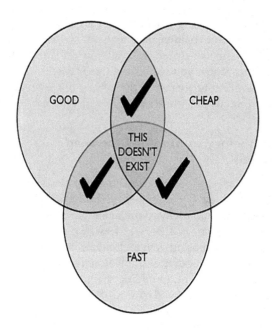

Figure 7.1 Reducing the need for traditional trade-offs through improving technology

- Use technology and innovation to deliver more with less, minimising the negative impacts of inevitable trade-offs.

Notes

1 Tomomi Yamane and Shinji Kaneko (March 2020) Millennials and generation Z are more sustainability-orientated – even when it comes to money, researchers find www.hiroshima-u.ac.jp/en/news/63924 [November 2021]
2 Prof Sarah Sayce FRICS, Fiona Quinn (October 2013) Sustainability and commercial property valuation www.rics.org/globalassets/rics-website/media/upholding-professional-standards/sector-standards/valuation/sustainability-and-commercial-property-valuation-2nd-edition-rics.pdf [November 2021]
3 Ian Malden and Becky Gaughan (June 2020) Property lenders moving towards awarding a 'green premium' for ESG-led real estate borrowing www.savills.co.uk/insight-and-opinion/savills-news/300973-0/property-

lenders-moving-towards-awarding-a–green-premium–for-esg-led-real-estate-borrowing [November 2021]

4 Green Energy Money (September 2016) Brown discounts & green premium value trends – new real estate market emerging risk www.greenenergy.money/brown-discounts-green-premium-value-trends-new-real-estate-market-emerging-risk/ [November 2021]

5 Smith, A. (2008) *An Inquiry into the Nature and Causes of the Wealth of Nations. Oxford World's Classics*. London, England: Oxford University Press.

6 UKGBC – Climate Change www.ukgbc.org/climate-change/ [November 2021]

7 National Federation of Builders Major Contractors Group (November 2019) Transforming construction for a low carbon future www.builders.org.uk/documents/transforming-construction-for-a-low-carbon-future/nfb-carbon-report-2019-online-webv2.pdf [November 2021]

8 Mark Solomons (January 2016) Which is the most hated company in Britain? New survey reveals all www.mirror.co.uk/news/uk-news/most-hated-company-britain-new-7199025 [November 2021]

9 Marshall Hargrave (July 2019) 'Obsolescence risk' definition www.investopedia.com/terms/o/obsolescenerisk.asp [November 2021]

8 How to improve operations

What you will learn

What needs to change around how you run your investments so that you are:

- *Running your investments professionally and compliantly,*
- *Incorporating innovations and*
- *Measuring both numerical and ESG targets*

Once you have made the strategic changes outlined in the previous part of this book, you need to optimise your operations. There's plenty of comprehensive books and guidance available on how to manage properties the traditional way. In this book, I'll focus on what needs to change. Why?

Well, divestment (selling properties to improve your overall portfolio performance) is not enough to get to net zero. We need technology and new innovations, policy and regulations, and we need private individuals and businesses to come up with solutions and new products with measurable impacts.

It's worth focusing on:

- Running your investments professionally and compliantly
- Incorporating innovations and
- Measuring both numerical and ESG targets

DOI: 10.1201/9781003196983-11

Running your investments professionally and compliantly

My hope is that readers of this book will already be doing their best to run their investments in a way that is professional and compliant. However, this is no easy task. As I have mentioned, at the time of writing, there are 168 laws and regulations guiding how investors run their portfolios and manage their properties.

The reality is, operating standards in the housing sector are inconsistent. Not every investor treats their investments like a business. So it's worth mentioning that this should be a priority. For example, well-meaning landlords might fail to have the necessary licence to let the property as a House in Multiple Occupation (HMO). They might serve an eviction notice incorrectly. They might not have enough (or working) smoke or carbon monoxide alarms. They might allow a damp or mould problem to continue to the point of health hazard.

The other reason this is relevant and important in the context of sustainable investments is that the UK government is particularly proactive in regulating the housing sector, both in terms of building standards and the operational side of properties. As a result, if you do nothing else from this book, as mentioned in the previous chapter, compliance is a solid baseline for more sustainable investment, socially and environmentally.

One known risk is that government policies and incentive schemes chop and change over the years. Compliance is of course necessary. That said, relying too heavily on one specific government scheme as a solution to the financial costs of compliance could be risky.

Keep an eye on what's next

Further public intervention in pursuit of sustainable investing is likely. This might take the form of government guidelines, new policies, laws and regulations targeting outcomes such as:

- Reducing emissions as part of our national efforts to achieve net zero

- Levelling up and reducing inequalities in living standards between regions
- Reducing inequalities and more equal housing opportunities between generations

For example, the Committee on Climate Change recommended government action around:

- Performance and compliance – In their view, the way new homes are built and existing homes retrofitted often falls short of design standards. This will mean greater levels of inspection and stricter enforcement of building standards and higher penalties for non-compliance. It might also entail stricter monitoring around existing properties.
- Skills gaps – For example, we need to plug a gap around low-carbon implementation, to correct for the lack of deployment skills for heat pumps.
- Retrofitting existing homes – There are 29 million existing homes across the UK, and improving their carbon and energy use is an infrastructure priority for the government (for example, through providing more subsidies and grants for energy-efficiency measures, such as loft and wall insulation).
- Building new homes – The 1.5 million new UK homes by 2022 that are planned will need to be low carbon, energy and water efficient and climate resilient. This is costly, though not as expensive as building cheap and retrofitting later. The committee recommended that from 2025 at the latest, no new homes should be connected to the gas grid; rather, they should be heated through low-carbon sources and have ultra-high levels of energy efficiency.
- Finance and funding – for example, for local authorities, in particular building control, and the Green Finance Task Force recommendations around green mortgages, green loans and fiscal incentives. As mentioned earlier, banks are increasingly willing and able to lend, and to do so more cheaply, on greener properties.

More broadly, new government policies are likely to include:

- Fiscal policy – for example, tax incentives to encourage upgrading existing buildings
- Education – which requires accurate measurement and assumes we know what to prioritise
- Legislation – for example, minimum EPC requirements
- Enforcement – for example, minimum maintenance requirements underpinning licencing and eviction legislation
- Nudge economics – which proposes positive reinforcement and indirect suggestions as ways to influence the behaviour and decision-making of groups or individuals

Proactively incorporating innovation

Innovations can make growing or running your portfolio quicker, cheaper or better. That said, as Bill Gates wisely put it in his excellent book *How to Avoid a Climate Disaster*, technology is 'necessary but not sufficient' for reducing the impacts of global warming.

You can improve outcomes in terms of financial and non-financial returns by:

- Improving ESG outcomes or impacts directly (for example, through smart building technologies)
- Using innovations to reduce running costs so that you can deliver more for less time and money and have the budget and bandwidth available to spend on making other ESG improvements without damaging your financial returns

Innovating to improve financial and non-financial outcomes and reduce running costs

There are many different types of innovation:

You can adjust existing technologies (including physical hardware and software) in existing markets incrementally, disrupt existing markets through using new technologies, apply existing technologies in new markets or radically establish new technologies in new markets, as illustrated previously.

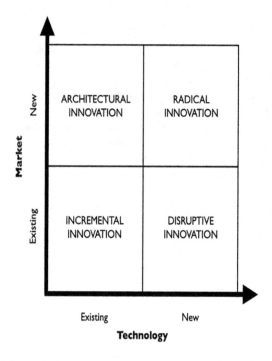

Figure 8.1 Innovation using new and existing technologies in new and existing markets

The reality for private investors is that it doesn't make sense to try to 'reinvent the wheel' or establish new technologies. This would be a distraction from your long-term goals of diversifying capital, protecting and growing wealth or earning additional investment income through bricks and mortar investment.

However, you should definitely consider incorporating incremental innovations and using new technologies, learning from innovators within and indeed beyond the real estate sector and spending time and effort on reviewing and upgrading the technologies you use to create and manage your portfolio or working with someone who is doing this.

What can we learn from other parts of the real estate sector to achieve more with less

The PRS tends to lag behind commercial property because the investors behind this sector have greater resourcing and more immediate commercial pressure to innovate. As a result, there is a lot we can learn from elsewhere. There is also a lot we can learn from proptech (another term for real estate technology or technologies) focused on residential property.

As a starter for ten (which I've kept mainly as high-level themes because new tech and innovative ideas are created all the time, and being too specific would date this book before it is published!), consider the potential positive impacts of:

- Digitising traditional processes so that you can analyse more data and access it online in real time (for example, property management and asset management software systems)
- Incorporating healthy living innovations (for example, air quality sensors)
- Using innovative 'contech' – the slightly dodgy-sounding name (sorry, but it's true!) for construction technology (for example, enhancements in construction materials and processes, such as 3D printing and modular building)
- Modern Methods of Construction – including offsite manufacturing and onsite alternatives to traditional house building, such as innovative techniques for laying concrete blockwork onsite to speed things up, limited on-site disruption and pollution and supply chain innovations (for example, Sweden now produces first steel carbon-free, using green hydrogen instead of the usual coal-fired blast furnace)
- Using internet of things (IoT) innovations – connected devices to transfer data without requiring human interaction. This includes using multiple devices, systems and/or digitised 'smart' buildings to improve efficiency and sustainability and using software to map out buildings, capture data and reduce energy usage through automatically controlling heating, ventilation, air conditioning, lighting, security and other systems

- Using new funding innovations which improve access, liquidity and ease of financing acquisitions or portfolio improvements
- Using connection platforms which link up buyers and sellers, owners and tenants, or construction parties and maintenance so that they can communicate, collaborate and share information more quickly and easily
- Incorporating sustainable innovations focused on the 'E' of ESG, such as energy savings, water efficiency and the 'circular economy', to sustain our natural resources, comply with new regulations or reduce costs (for example, on-site energy generation, water-reuse systems and waste minimisation and/or a closed-loop waste-management approach)
- Using virtual reality and 3D mapping to replicate an environment (for example, virtual viewings) or using drone technology or computers to create, plan, design and ultimately build, operate and maintain an (initially) alternative reality (for example, Building Information Modelling, or BIM)
- Using drones to assess the need for repairs to save money
- Using technology to understand and minimise carbon emissions – This is not just about paying money to offset emissions, and it's not just about imposing technology on existing properties. It pays to follow a process. The UK Green Building Council explains five steps to follow:

  - Establish the scope of net zero carbon – whether this is for construction or operational energy
  - Reduce construction impacts (where relevant)
  - Reduce operational energy use – For example, in residential properties, we need electric heat pumps to replace gas boilers; much better insulation of old houses, including new doors and windows; and much better lining/lagging and tree and hedge planting to suck up carbon
  - Increase renewable energy supply
  - Offset any remaining carbon

So, it is first about improving energy efficiency then shifting to renewable energy supplies and only offsetting as a last resort.

Investing is not an isolated activity. It's tied up with other activities such as development and technology. Private investors can learn a lot from what is happening elsewhere.

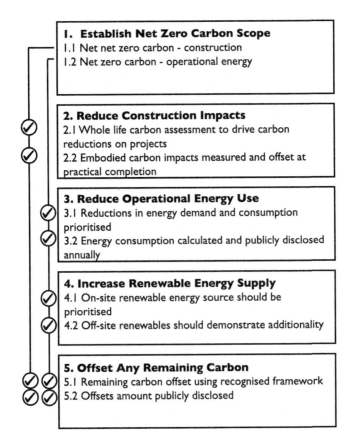

Figure 8.2 Steps to achieving a net zero carbon building

Source: Emily Huynh (March 2021) Renewable energy procurement & carbon offsetting. London: UK Green Building Council. www.ukgbc.org/wp-content/uploads/2021/03/Renewable-Energy-Procurement-Carbon-Offsetting-Guidance-for-Net-Zero-Carbon-Buildings.pdf

As mentioned earlier, technology is becoming obsolete faster. As a result, investors need to continually educate themselves on what technologies are available to them or seek regular advice from the experts.

Measuring financial and ESG impacts

Measurement is vital because 'you can't manage what you don't measure'.

Profit and other financial metrics are easy to measure using traditional accounting tools and practices. Adding sustainability into the mix makes it much harder.

John Elvington coined the memorable and much-used phrase 'triple bottom line' when discussing how we can measure the three key elements of sustainable investing: people, planet, profit. Many other approaches followed, from carbon productivity to environmental, social and governance frameworks.[1]

The 'bewildering range of options' is the main reason why Elvington proposed he 'carry out a management concept recall' on the concept's 25th anniversary.[2]

The wide range of possible approaches provided an 'alibi for inaction' and made it difficult to benchmark progress in terms of real-world impact and performance. The large number of possible approaches and the cost of using them can quickly lead to overwhelming people, inaction and a bias in favour of what seems easier, cheaper or more familiar, such as measuring profit and nothing else. It can also create the risk of greenwashing.

This is a market-wide issue. The vast array of available options stymies individual investors since there are few consistent, credible, commonly accepted and, at the same time, commercially viable approaches. This final point is important because, as mentioned, this is not about charity. However, many aspects of sustainable impact are expensive to measure and process, in particular for diverse housing stock and tenant types. If measurement costs £50,000 each year and your annual profit was £30,000, then measurement is just not commercially viable.

Measuring environmental and social impacts can be even more difficult for private investors, who don't have the luxury of teams of analysts to support them. There are advantages to scale, and the literature suggests there is a bias against small- and medium-sized enterprises in this regard.

Numerical approach based on lag or lead indicators

As the innovations mentioned previously highlight, one of the most impactful solutions affecting real estate is figuring out how to measure sustainable investing. However, innovation alone is not enough.

To remove the emotional dimension and facilitate good decision-making, you need a step-by-step process based on numerical values.

You can use lag indicators or lead indicators.

Lag indicators are:

> an observable or measurable factor that changes some time after the economic, financial, or business variable it is correlated with changes. Lagging indicators confirm trends and changes in trends.[3]

For example, you might measure improvements in environmental efficiency of built assets or improvements in tenant satisfaction.

Lead indicators are:

> any measurable or observable variable of interest that predicts a change or movement in another data series, process, trend, or other phenomenon of interest before it occurs.[4]

For example, you might measure the budget you allocate towards environmental upgrades to buildings or response times to tenant maintenance enquiries.

Lead indicators are often easier and more cost-effective. This is important for private investors.

For example, you might focus on easily measurable key worker housing discounts. This is easier and likely to be more accurate than measuring improvements in ability to employ key workers in a local hospital. The latter would be complicated, cost ineffective and influenced by many other factors and therefore potentially also misleading.

Whether you choose to focus on lag or lead indicators, you ideally want to attach a numerical value to your impacts so that you can quickly make decisions without bias, and you need to set and measure against clear targets.

For example, let's say your average EPC rating is D, and in fact you have an even split in terms of ratings: 20% of your portfolio is F and 20% is E, D, C and B. You might place a higher impact value on improvements from F to C than on improvements from C to A because the marginal impact of this will be greater.

If you just want to measure a snapshot and have a clear, simple target to achieve in the next 5 years, you might simply set a target of an average rating of B.

If you want to optimise the process for maximum impact up front, you might give yourself 100 points for every rating uplift for properties that fall below D currently and 50 points for every rating uplift for properties rated C or above currently.

This would be helpful for you in allocating your resources to align with where regulations and valuations are going and the emergence of the brown discount mentioned previously.

You should also consider your timeframe for investment. For example, let's say your EPC highlights you could save £10 per year on electricity bills by purchasing a £15 draft excluder (also known as 'door snakes' – these are cheap but effective strips of foam rubber, metal or other material inserted in a door or window frame to keep out draughts). The relative return on investment (how much you make or save relative to the pounds outlaid – for example, £10 per year on energy bills over a £15 investment would give you a 67% return on investment) is strong. The absolute return is not (in the example provided, you only save £10). Whilst you can try to incentivise tenants to make such changes, unfortunately, energy bill savings can sometimes be immaterial in relation to the cost to your tenant, which means such investments are largely up to you.

The same assessment might highlight that you could install solar panels that would save you £300 per year. But the cost is £15,000. The rational, profit-motivated investor in the short to medium term (1–3 years) would choose the draft excluder. If, instead, you look at the longer term (for example, 20+ years), care enough about environmental impact to accept a longer-term payback period and are not prohibited by the absolute cost, you might choose the latter.

The previous decision might be influenced not just by the improvement to EPC rating associated but also by the positive image improvement from being seen to be more sustainable. How does the improvement make you feel, and how does it make you look to suppliers, creditors, investors and tenants? You need to be able to attach a numerical value to this, too, since you might not get a lot of kudos for buying a draft excluder, but having solar panels might have a substantial impact on the value and saleability of the property.

Such considerations are essential rather than 'nice to do'. Whether investors feel good about it or not (hopefully they do), sustainable features will have an increasingly big impact on valuations and capital (affecting your ability to source equity and debt), not to mention mandatory regulatory requirements and income security (your ability to retain tenants paying rent).

The point is you need to be able to break things down numerically. You need a decision-making framework that considers the time frame. You need to understand what the absolute and relative impacts will be worth to you as an investor. This will enable you to make better-informed decisions that align with the goal of preserving and growing your wealth with positive impacts.

We are reliant on technology and innovation or grants for improvement works for measurement to be commercially viable. The good news is, we live in a data-driven age. AI and algorithms can quickly and efficiently process information, and there's a big opportunity to leverage data and digital methods for better monitoring and more informed decision-making.

Top tips

- Use technology to improve financial and non-financial outcomes.
- Use technology to reduce costs so that you have more budget to allocate to improving ESG outcomes.
- Spend time and effort getting to know what resources are out there, or you need to work with someone who does.

- Conduct regular (for example, annual or biannual) reviews of your portfolio and its performance and what new technologies are worth incorporating.
- Use lag and lead indicators with a numerical approach to measure ESG impacts aligned with your values.
- Use numerical indicators to guide your decisions.
- Check out the following for inspiration on measurement:

  - https://gresb.com/about/
  - www.breeam.com/discover/resources/
  - www.buildcarbonneutral.org/

Notes

1 Other approaches include Double and Quadruple Bottom Lines, Social Return on Investment (SROI), multiple capital models, Full Cost Accounting, Environmental, Social and Governance (ESG), Environmental Profit & Loss, Net Positive, Blended and Shared Value, Integrated Reporting, Impact Investment, Total Societal Impact framework, Carbon Productivity, the Sharing and Circular Economies, or Biomimicry.
2 John Elkington (June 2018) 25 Years ago I coined the phrase 'triple bottom line'. Here's why it's time to rethink it https://hbr.org/2018/06/25-years-ago-i-coined-the-phrase-triple-bottom-line-heres-why-im-giving-up-on-it [November 2021]
3 Charles Potters and Daniel Rathburn (May 2021) Lagging indicator definition www.investopedia.com/terms/l/laggingindicator.asp [November 2021]
4 Michael J. Boyle and Ariel Courage (February 2021) Leading indicator definition www.investopedia.com/terms/l/leadingindicator.asp [November 2021]

9 Two common operational mistakes and how to avoid them

What you will learn

- *Common mistakes and how to avoid them, including:*
    - *Being unprofessional or non-compliant*
    - *Not measuring results*

To avoid the costs and risks of getting it wrong, it makes sense not to repeat common operational mistakes. This chapter shares examples so that you can avoid them.

Mistake #4: Being unprofessional or non-compliant

For obvious reasons, being unprofessional or non-compliant is risky. The mistake to avoid is not considering either current or anticipated future standards properly and not factoring in the cost of rectification or compliance, such as:

- Gas safety checks
- Smoke and carbon monoxide alarms
- EPCs
- Tenancy deposits – which you must protect correctly and before which you must serve the 'prescribed information'
- Landlord selective licenses or licenses for HMOs
- Furniture and furnishings safety regulations
- Fire safety compliance such as ESW1 and Fire Risk Assessments
- Electrical safety standards inspections/reports

DOI: 10.1201/9781003196983-12

Why is it a mistake?

For investors, not complying with regulations can lead to significant fines, rent payback orders and even criminal convictions, legal battles and imprisonment.

For example, your local council can issue a civil penalty of up to £30,000. They don't even need to take you to court. Your details could be entered on a national 'rogues database'. You could be banned from letting property. In the most serious cases, such as injury, death of a tenant or multiple offences, you could even be criminally convicted and face jail time. Following a government consultation over fire safety in multiple-occupancy properties prompted by the Grenfell tragedy, the Home Office announced that there are plans to introduce unlimited fines for landlords and managing agents of HMO who breach fire safety regulations under the Building Safety Bill.[1] You may also lose control of your property since a simple mistake in the tenant onboarding process can mean you are unable to legally evict the tenant should you need to.

There is a risk of unforeseen costs hampering your profit margins if you fail to factor in the cost of compliance with policy. For example, at the time of writing, many investors (and homeowners) are being forced into precarious financial positions as the cost of temporary security measures to prevent the risk of fires are deemed necessary in buildings which have not been able to provide a satisfactory EWS1 certificate. Industry press and investor blogs regularly share horror stories of rogue landlords who disregard the law and are punished for it.

Being unprofessional or not complying with laws is also problematic because not complying raises the possibility of providing unsafe homes, which directly affects human lives.

How you can avoid it

Big change tends to be led by the government and can include both 'carrots' (for example, grants) and 'sticks' (for example, fines for non-compliance with regulations). As I've mentioned, there's currently 168 laws and regulations affecting property and its management, and you need to stay on top of these or hire an expert who can.

For many years, people thought that property investment was easy. I don't agree. It might be relatively simple, but it's far from easy.

To avoid the financial and social risks of non-compliance, factor in the cost of aligning with regulations, including:

- Improving the fabric of your properties (for example, in terms of environmental efficiency if your properties have low EPC ratings)
- Paying attention to suggested maintenance items pointed out in your building surveys or Fire Risk Assessments
- Factoring in the costs of professional management – whether in-house or outsourced. Yes, you could probably do it yourself, but that frequently leads to inefficient or substandard results. Unless you're already in the property management business, you may need to change how you operate to be confident that you'll do a professional job.
- Making sure your manager is on top of new regulations, because they are coming thick and fast
- Treating – or ensuring that your manager is treating – your tenants as you would want family and friends to be treated in terms of professionalism and compliance

On your management, there are two ways of making sure you have the capacity to deal with the burden of compliance and professionalism:

1 Scale up and create more efficiencies, use technology and work with the right teams, contractors or staff and systems to ensure things are well-managed, risks are managed, mitigated and minimised, and the sustainability potential of your portfolio is met.
2 Partner with or hire professionals, or invest indirectly (for example, via an REIT).

The direction of travel is that landlords need to treat their investments as a professional business, not a sideline hobby, in order to be both compliant and competitive. For example, from a tax perspective, Section 24 means that it makes sense to invest via a limited company rather than in your personal name. The costs associated with this (for example, annual accounts) mean it makes less sense for small portfolios. It is increasingly inefficient to own a portfolio of fewer than five properties for most private investors.

You can use technologies, including some of those mentioned in earlier chapters, to help you create and manage your portfolio. You can also work with or invest through specialists, including:

- REITs – These are more liquid, though less stable in terms of value than direct real estate investments. You have neither the control nor the responsibility of investing directly. Some are diversified, owning commercial and residential properties. Others are specialist (for example, focused solely on student housing or PRS investments).
- Crowdfunding – Crowdfunded equity gives you neither the control nor the responsibility of investing directly. For projects involving development, the potential returns can be attractive; however, the risks are a lot higher. For 'buy and hold' investments, the returns are typically lower than you would get investing directly. This is because there are lots of costs to pay, but the scale of such portfolios and projects is generally not high enough for the efficiencies of scale available to REITs.
- Private equity and family offices – These tend to have a high cost base. They are used to investments offering higher risk and higher return than most long-term residential investments offer. Further, your capital will likely be tied up for a long time.
- Scaling up alone – a great option if you have the specialist knowledge and networks required. Investors tend to fall down when investing alone is through getting the set-up wrong for a long-term investment; making emotional rather than strategic decisions; not having access to attractive opportunities; not being able to filter down potential investments effectively and acquiring the wrong kind of assets for sustainable investment;

not managing their portfolio in a way that is professional, compliant or cost-effective; and making urgent rather than strategic, profit-maximising decisions around their exit.

Top tips

- Be aware of the increasing importance of compliance – to manage your own risks and bottom line and for the safety and happiness of your tenants.
- Scale up and create more efficiencies, or partner with or hire professionals.

Mistake #5: Not measuring results

There is a market-wide problem with finding consistent, credible, commercially viable and commonly accepted methods of measuring ESG impacts.

This creates a problem for you as an investor.

You can measure financial value via traditional RICS valuations and environmental building quality via EPCs. The RICS motto is 'Est modus in rebus' – measure in all things. It turns out this is easier said than done. Even the traditional RICS financial valuation can vary wildly between one valuer and the next. So what happens when you add in complex environmental and social considerations such as community benefits and the dynamism of improvements over time on top of the simplistic bricks and mortar snapshots used currently? What would you measure to reflect a snapshot or improvement in social value? Ideally, you need to incorporate improvements in environmental, social and community value for dynamic, multi-dimensional assessment, but this is far from easy.

Why is it a mistake?

Measurement is your problem because as mentioned:

you can't manage what you can't measure.

The right kind of measurement can actually help you to achieve financial and non-financial goals. In fact, the 'mere-measurement effect' suggests that simply measuring intentions can improve performance.[2]

It is very difficult to know if you're on track without having a way to keep track of progress. To achieve the benefits of sustainable investing and to avoid inefficient, ineffective allocations of resources, waste and undesirable environmental and social costs, measurement is essential.

How you can avoid this mistake

Ultimately, there is a need for market-wide solutions. To overcome the problem of measurement requires collaboration between investors, tenants, regulators and trade bodies due to the increasing number of new regulations and minimum standards.

Since you can't collaborate on your own, in the meantime, you can follow some simple steps.

1   Decide what to measure – what will be viable, and aligned with your priorities?
2   Decide how you can measure these impacts – work out a way of measuring, using lag and lead indicators and a numerical approach so that you can easily assess progress.
3   Take action anyway – the real benefit of measurement is that it enables you to manage and improve results. Don't let an inability to measure the impact prevent you from trying to invest in a way that is more sustainable. Instead, you can manage improvements yourself by investing in line with principles, controlling the inputs rather than fully understanding the outcomes.

Firstly, decide what to measure based on your mission and goals. Is it about offsetting emissions through trees planted or affordability and security measured through discounts or rent:income ratios?

Secondly, consider and research what you can measure using current technologies. Wherever possible, incorporate technology to improve, measure or manage ESG improvements. Measurement is becoming easier with more tools at our disposal. We now have access to more data than ever, and the ability to quickly interpret it via algorithms and artificial intelligence (AI). There is a huge opportunity to leverage around data and digital information for better monitoring and informed decision-making. Given the complexities, currently it's well-worth hiring an expert to help.

Consider both lead indicators (proxies such as discounts given rather than affordability, or spend on improvements – which are typically cheaper and easier to track) and lag indicators which show concrete impacts. Use a numerical approach, as outlined earlier, where this is possible.

Check out examples of what others are doing. For example, in social housing, we have the Social Reporting Standard report. Carbon tracking, energy auditing, life cycle assessments and the kind of mandatory greenhouse gas reporting used by FTSE main market companies are also worth looking into. Check out the sustainability or environmental reports used by leading construction businesses to support and complement their annual report and accounts. There are also organisations to help measure social value like the Social Value Portal, who work with over 80 government agencies.

Net zero audits can be used to understand the cost of retrofitting and how it compares with your rental income and, therefore, at what point it is commercially viable. However, this is relatively new; it is only just becoming possible to work this cost into analyses. Further, net zero audits are not consistent. That's why it can make more sense to focus on taking action anyway.

Thirdly, if you decide to take action and manage outcomes without measurement, you should decide on some clear principles for the elements you can control.

For example, you could use only FSC certified timber, low-carbon concrete, well-fitted, quality insulation, on-site energy generation, smart meters and electric car charge points. Measuring inputs like this rather than focusing on outcomes can be cheaper and can lead to similar results as there is a limit on what you can adjust anyway, in particular for existing buildings. You might want to focus on freehold houses or multi-unit flat blocks since it can be difficult to improve the quality (for example, windows or building insulation) of a single flat in a block where you are not the freeholder.

Let's say the social impact you want to have is about improving and 'upcycling' bricks and mortar assets. You could measure the impact on EPC ratings from works (which have to be measured every 10 years anyway to comply with regulations) as a lag indicator. You could measure improvement spending as a lead indicator. Or you could rely on data from other people's projects to give you confidence that planned upgrades would have a clear positive impact on environmental factors such as emissions.

Using measurement to understand what to do with your portfolio

I mentioned earlier that one of the major problems in the housing market is that the cost of retrofitting can be high. For older properties, it can sometimes be better to knock down and start again, which comes at a cost.

To work out what to do and how, you need to be confident on your investment strategy and timeframes, and you need accurate, appropriate measurement of the performance of your properties and the costs and benefits of retrofitting or starting again.

For example, let's say you have a portfolio of tired Victorian properties with average EPC ratings of E. Easy, cheap and quick ways to enhance performance include getting draft excluders, and you can use the recommendations in your EPC to guide the easy steps. You could also improve insulation in the walls, roof and windows (although, as mentioned, this could have negative impacts on your tenants – for example, creating ventilation issues that cause asthma – like a sticking plaster preventing your skin from breathing).

Realistically though, the properties are never going to be rated A for environmental performance no matter how much you spend. The average EPC of English housing has improved from E to D, but there are still many properties that are D or below, as illustrated in Figure 9.1.

What's more, the cost of retrofitting the building can be expensive. Sometimes, it can make more sense to knock a building down

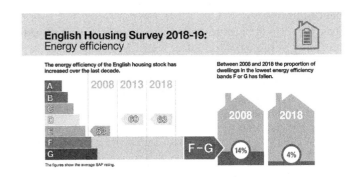

Figure 9.1 Energy efficiency of English housing

Source: Ministry of Housing, Communities &and Local Government (July 2020) English housing survey energy efficiency, 2018–19 https://assets.publishing.service.gov.uk/government/uploads/system/uploads/attachment_data/file/898344/Energy_Report.pdf [November 2021]

and start again. There are financial and environmental costs of this, too. You would need to calculate these costs to work out when and whether this is the more viable option. This will depend on how long the property has been left: where it is in its life cycle. From an environmental perspective, you'd want to calculate the carbon output of continuing to run the property over the coming years (for example, what is the operational carbon output over the next 10, 20 or 30 years?). How does this compare with the carbon cost of knocking down and restarting (the end-of-life and embodied carbon costs)? For properties with less than 30 years of usable life, for example, it might make more sense to demolish and start again. Before making changes, you must also consider the social impact of altering buildings. For example if you need to re-house tenants this will not only affect investment income, but will disrupt the lives of your tenants.

Right now, this probably doesn't make sense for you from a commercial perspective. However, in years to come, as environmental sustainability is more heavily priced into our existing housing stock, less efficient properties will become increasingly cheap relative to more efficient properties. It's likely that grants and tax credits ('carrots') and taxation and regulations ('sticks') will also influence this.

Over time it will become easier, with more attention placed on sustainability in property, to look at your investment life cycle and the performance of your properties and to calculate the commercial and financial costs and benefits and the time horizon needed for the work you are considering. It will also become easier to understand how it will pay off over your planned investment timeframe.

Top tips

- Decide what to measure – aligning with your priorities and what is viable.
- Decide how to measure, using lag or lead indicators.
- Use a numerical approach to make it easier to base decisions on the results of measurement.
- Take action anyway, investing in line with certain principles and making adjustments known to improve outcomes.

Notes

1 Department for Levelling Up, Housing and Communities and Ministry of Housing, Communities & Local Government (July 2021) Building safety bill www.gov.uk/government/collections/building-safety-bill [November 2021]
2 Vicki G. Morwitz and Gavan J. Fitzsimons (2004) The mere-measurement effect: Why does measuring intentions change actual behavior www.sciencedirect.com/science/article/abs/pii/S1057740804701333 [November 2021]

10 Summary/conclusion

What you will learn

- *What we covered and why it's relevant and important for you*
- *What you can do next*

The mission

The goal of this book is to give private investors the information and tools needed to understand what sustainable residential property investing is and how to shift to a more sustainable model of investing.

It's about empowering residential investors like you to adjust your approach to align with the times we are in so that ultimately, you can create positive impacts whilst making attractive returns. Ultimately, it's about improving your long-term returns and the resilience of those returns and limiting the costs and risks of being too late or being behind the curve.

What we've covered

I started by explaining how UK residential property continues to attract national and international attention. I explained the differences between property investing and property ownership and property investing and other forms of investing.

Next, I highlighted how, for many years, property investing has offered a solution to you if you want to protect and grow wealth

DOI: 10.1201/9781003196983-13

and feel rewarded, make profits and have a tangible impact you can be proud of, in a way that is relatively easy to understand and implement.

The fundamentals of supply and demand drive strong past performance and future forecasts for residential property. The unique attraction, simplicity and accessibility of property has created a fragmented market. The trouble is, the combination of diverse ownership and aging housing stock creates a challenge for sustainability.

This is not the only important market change. I explained key changes such as:

- Political shifts, including the uncertainty associated with Brexit and Covid-19, and a more consumer-focused political agenda
- Economic trends, including long-term low interest rates stimulating demand and unemployment limiting affordability for potential property buyers
- Social trends, including demographic changes, affordability constraints and rising living standards. These trends create growing demand for rental housing. People living alone for longer also increase demand for yield-focused investments from pension funds/individuals planning for retirement.
- Technological advances, innovation and data, which create the potential for investment to be more efficient, accessible and sustainable, making it is easier to monitor and manage progress
- Legal and regulatory changes, including recent regulations, shift the balance of power from smaller investors and sideline landlords and broadly align with a more consumer-focused political agenda.
- Environmental awareness and the growing requirement to protect the planet, including through the UK's commitment to net zero

Due to these recent market changes, whilst residential assets remain attractive, the old ways of investing are broken. As a result, now is a great time to reconsider and reshape all aspects of investing, from ownership structures to sustainability and impact.

Next I explained what sustainable investing is, how to integrate sustainability into investing, what sustainable residential investing is and what it isn't and why it is so important, as a way to improve outcomes, reduce risks and solve problems for profit-motivated investors, people and the planet. Sustainable investing has many definitions, frameworks and approaches, which can quickly become overwhelming.

In the second part of the book, I shared a simple framework for sustainable investing.

First, I outlined the strategic changes required. This is about adapting your mission, setting clear targets aligned with that mission and understanding and accepting the trade-offs. It is all about identifying the right kind of investments to make at the right prices. The idea is that you can identify what a good deal looks like, what to invest in and what to divest of, as well as understand the timeframes for investing and how your payback period may change.

We covered common mistakes to avoid, in particular:

- Thinking ESG is a fad you don't need to worry about
- Setting the wrong targets and timeframes or not pricing in what's next
- Not prioritising and misunderstanding the trade-offs

Next I outlined how to optimise your operations. This section is about running your investments professionally and compliantly, incorporating innovations, learning from others and measuring both numerical and ESG targets.

I highlighted common mistakes and how you can avoid them, including:

- Being unprofessional or non-compliant
- Not measuring results

It should be clear by now that there is no perfect answer.

Avoiding the less favourable options in relation to sustainability requires:

- Clear understanding – of the importance of sustainability and how to invest in a way that is sustainable commercially, environmentally and socially

- The right strategies focused on the right goals
- Operational compliance, innovative approaches and products, and accurate measurement and management

The truth is, for long-term investors in UK residential property, profit maximisation is no longer the only consideration. Your investments must increasingly be profitable as well as sustainable: economically resilient with positive ESG metrics. These can deliver benefits, including potential improvements to cash flow, wealth preservation and value growth that come with the rising importance of sustainability. Not investing sustainably can be costly and risky.

The trouble is, there is no perfect approach. Perhaps the best we can do is avoid the worst (for example, avoiding the mistakes I've highlighted previously).

As a private investor, you can only make a difference to what you control. This is also the opportunity. It will take longer, and it won't be easy, but collectively, private investors can make a big difference given the percentage of housing stock owned by individuals.

Printed in the United States
by Baker & Taylor Publisher Services